SUPREME EXIT

Florence Ballard After Motown

Shawniqua Nychole Williamson-Smith

Uno 220
Kom Poo Pie Publishing, LLC.

Supreme Exit

Copyright © 2021 Shawniqua Nychole Williamson-Smith. All rights reserved. No part of this publication may be reproduced or transmitted in any form or by any means, electronic, mechanical, photocopying, recording, or otherwise, without the prior written permission of the publisher, except in the case of brief quotations embodied in reviews and certain other non-commercial uses permitted by copyright law. This book is not meant to offend anyone, as it deals with a lot of sensitive issues that many people struggle with, and often need more help than a book can offer. It may be therapeutic, but this book does not replace real therapy. This book is meant only for educational and informational purposes and should not be considered therapy or any other form of treatment. If you think you need immediate assistance, call your local emergency number or the mental health crisis hotline listed in your phone book's government pages. Seek specialized training and professional judgment of a health care or mental health care professional. The author is not able to respond to specific comments or questions about personal situations, appropriate diagnosis or treatment, or otherwise, provide any clinical opinions; further, the author is not liable if the reader relied on the material and was financially damaged in some way. Although the author and publisher have made every effort to ensure that the information in this book was correct at press time, the author and publisher do not assume and hereby disclaim any liability to any party for any loss, damage, or disruption caused by errors or omissions, whether such errors or omissions result from negligence, accident, or any other cause.

- Requests for permission to make copies of any part of the work should be submitted to the publisher, Kom Poo Pie Publishing, LLC.: kompoopie@gmail.com
- Printed in the United States of America
- First Printing: July 2020
- ISBN: 978-1-7349829-3-0
- LCCN: 2020908118

DEDICATION

Supreme Exit is dedicated to all of the many dedicated fans of the one and only beloved Florence Glenda Ballard Chapman. Yes! This book is dedicated to you. You are special; you are of great importance, and you matter. You are why Florence's legacy is that much more relevant. My heart was full witnessing the undying love you all exude for a woman who honestly loved you all just as much. You all were a part of some of Florence's highest and happiest moments in her lifetime. She never forgot about you. She felt a constant responsibility to please you all, and aimed to bless you with more of her sultry vocal talents. Thank you for everything you do to keep Florence's memory alive.

    I dedicate this book to you in honor of Florence, on behalf of the impact she left on us. Only you know what Florence meant to you. The feeling is one of pure love that will always be a place to visit and enjoy as you please. Continue to connect with Florence through her music and her words, or whatever way you do. Whatever the memory or moment is, or was, for you, will forever be, and no one can take that from you. Let this inspire you and all of us to impact others in such a way through our own lifetimes.

    Love should be shared, not spared. Remember, 'Love Ain't Love' until you give it.

CONTENTS

Preface 9

CHAPTER UNO: FLORENCE 13
    Borrowed Time 13
    A Fishy Tale 17
    Smell the Smoke - Feel the Burn 21
    Does Time Heal All Wounds? 23
    Dr. Jekyll, What Are You Hiding? 26
    Stop the Clock 32
    Tick Tock 37
    Slow Motion 43
    The Unreachable 46
    The Final Curtain Call 48
    The Untouchables 52
    Forever Faithful 53
    Florence Ballard Chapman Through Nicole's Eyes 56

CHAPTER DOS: TOMMY 59
    Not-So-Lucky Number Seven 60
    I'm All Yours Until Tomorrow 65
    The Rape of Nicole Chapman 67

 The Rape of Florence Ballard 70
 Who Was Reggie Harding? 71
 The Graystone 75
 I Will Survive 77
 A Boost 79
 Another Big Loss 80

CHAPTER TRES: NICOLE 85
 My Way 87
 Finding Love 88
 Level Up 91
 In Other Words 92
 Lobbying for a Hobby 93
 Say What You Mean and Mean What You Say 95
 Change Gone Come 99
 Recognizing Flo' After Death 102
 Peace and Blessings 103
 Love and Support to the Max 110
 The Book Max Wrote 111
 Aunt Pat 111
 Listen, Linda 113
 Assumptions 116
 Mental Health 117
 Love Ain't Love 119
 Where Did the Money Go? 120

CHAPTER CUATRO:
SETTING THE RECORD STRAIGHT 123
    Broken Leg 123
    Urban Legend 124
    Correction 125

CHAPTER CINCO: NICOLE'S MENTIONS 127
    Charles in Charge 127
    Faith Evans 128
    Flavor Flav 130
    Raymond Gibson 131
    Jennifer Hudson 132
    Berry Gordy, Jr. 132

Florence 135
The Impossible Dream 137
Acknowledgments 143
The Fans 146
Nicholas Lamont Stiles 147
Jim Saphin 148
References 149
Credits 151
About the Author 153
Who is Uno 220? 153
Florence Ballard Chapman Speaks 155
Happy Heavenly 77th Birthday 157
Florence Glenda Ballard Chapman 157

PREFACE

How did this book come to be?

In 2015, I was called to partner on a film project as executive producer, under the direction of Jay Lamont of "Ball Out Boy Films." He was contacted by Florence Ballard Chapman's grandson, De'Juan, to produce a film telling the story of his grandmother's life from his mother and other family and close friends' memories. De'Juan introduced me to his mom, Nicole Chapman, and her twin sister Michelle. The twins are deeply passionate and protective of their mother's legacy. Michelle and Nicole explained that they had dealings with other prospects that did not work out as planned. The other prospects were not who they claimed to be, and proved to be fraudulent. This caused Michelle and Nicole to be apprehensive about any other offers. Michelle shared her concerns with me, making it clear that she had no interest in being scammed again, no matter how good the proposal sounded.

During the initial interviews for the film's script, other family members and friends had much information to share. Over time, the meetings trimmed down to Nicole Chapman and me only. With all of the pertinent details of her mom's life collected by me, my questioning came to a close, and a few months later, the script was complete. I worked on the script throughout the interview sessions, but upon the finalization of the script, *In the Name of Love*, I felt a sense of redundancy with the project in hand.

Although the script shared new information, it was not enough to balance out the story. I felt the story needed something different added, which stagnated the work and led to the film not being produced. Instead, I meditated some nights while listening to Florence sing, trying to tap into her journey and the messages she attempted to share with the world.

Suddenly, I felt my interest shift more toward Florence, the mother, than Florence, the singer. I felt it was imperative to tell the parts of her life that were missing in all of the other stories being told for over the past forty years. The interview sessions between Nicole and I sparked again, but this time I took a different approach, by adding Nicole's life to her mom's story as it results in the loss of her mother at a young age. Nicole agreed to the book idea, and the real work began.

Most of the information given through these sets of interviews gave pause, as some of the shocking information had to do with Florence, while much more mounted on Nicole. There was so much to tell, and Nicole was ready to tell it all. I became emotionally connected and invested in the life Nicole lived. I decided to write and publish the book first, then release the movie that tells Florence's experience as a wife, mother, daughter, sister, aunt, friend, and more, all through Nicole's eyes.

Nicole has been eager to tell her mother's story, her way. Throughout the interviews, Nicole also shared memories of her life after her mom passed. Nicole's story is one that I feel the fans of her mom would appreciate her sharing. Nicole wants her mother's fans to know who her mother was after Motown, and how complex her life became. This story continues with intimate details of Nicole's life with her parents and after their passing.

Nychole & Nicole

Nicole and I communicate well with respect, love, and understanding. Patience was key for this project, since Nicole had to relive her youth, including the most painful moments in her life. To trust me with intimate information that Nicole had never given to anyone else was heavy. I promised to carry the weight and tell her mother's story the way she wants it told.

Nicole also wants her mother, Florence Glenda Ballard Chapman, honored properly, acknowledged, and celebrated. Nicole has dreamed of one day seeing a film in honor of her mom from her description. I have accepted the duty of bringing these dreams to life, and much more.

CHAPTER UNO

FLORENCE

Florence Glenda (Ballard) Chapman, born June 30, 1943, and died February 22, 1976.

Borrowed Time

In three short days, Nicole Chapman will be a motherless child. She didn't know any other children that didn't have a mom, so the thought of waking up motherless so young never crossed her mind. When you say goodnight, it should last the entire night, but February 20th, 1976, wasn't a good night for any of them inside Florence Chapman's home.

Nicole remembers the day starting as normal as any other day. Florence's weekday routine always began with waking the girls up for school, getting them dressed, tending to baby, Lisa, and making breakfast. Their dad was an early riser and always up and ready before them. Tommy was a handsome, well-dressed and put together man. Some describe his way of dressing as quite dapper. Some mornings Tommy would eat a light breakfast, like a fried egg over easy with toast and coffee at the table alongside his daughters and wife. Other times he would just have coffee and read the newspaper at or near the table until his twin daughters, Nicole and Michelle, were finished eating and ready to go to school. Reading the newspaper was his solitude every morning before his work shift began. Tommy worked as a full-time driver for Berry Gordy, Jr. and many others assigned by Gordy himself.

Tommy was his daughter's personal driver as well. Nicole and Michelle were chauffeured to and from school every day in his black Cadillac. Nicole riding with her father to school every morning was like hearing the same song at the same time everyday. The daily repetitive rhythm went like this: start the car, turn on the radio, back out of the driveway, then drive off while he was lighting his joint, which is cannabis rolled with translucent paper. Yes, Tommy smoked marijuana (weed) in the car every morning while driving his twin daughters to school. This was not Tommy's only time to smoke his weed, but it was definitely a committed time. Nicole remembers her mother not liking her father Tommy smoking weed, and that he was not allowed to do so in the house, even though it was cool for Florence to smoke her Kool Menthol cigarettes inside the home and car. Back in 1976, no one made much of a fuss about people smoking in front of children. This was before second-hand smoke became a well-known issue.

Marijuana was considered a gateway drug in the 1970s. Gateway meaning that marijuana usage could likely lead the marijuana smoker into using a heavier drug. There were vague rumors of Tommy experimenting with cocaine as well, but it has never been confirmed for Nicole. Maybe all these statistical measures made Florence feel her actions against weed were fair. Maybe Tommy felt the only time he could smoke before starting his day every morning would be during the girls' ride to school. Nicole never said anything about this to anyone. It was not because she felt it was wrong, merely because she did not speak much about what her parents did behind closed doors to anyone.

She will never forget how much her daddy loved his weed. She remembers seeing him sneak to the basement to smoke sometimes. She believes the weed helped her father relieve stress. He never knew his daughter's awareness was so keen. Nicole laughed as she recalled this. She mentioned, "She was not offended by this, then, as she is not now." There were never any alarming behavioral changes in her father after he smoked his weed. "Tommy smoking marijuana never affected his daughter negatively and if it did, but went unnoticed, so be it. It was what it was and is what it is," quoted Nicole.

Tommy was known to be a cool, calm, and collected type of guy. It was not often that his buttons were pushed, but when they were, it was his wife Florence doing the pushing. Tommy was a cool guy to associate with. He was easy-going, but not a pushover by any means. Nicole always felt safe and protected around her dad. She knew no one would hurt her, or they would get hurt by her dad. She felt like she had a personal bodyguard chauffeuring her around. She saw a lot of the bodyguard lifestyle growing up around other celebrities. Getting the girls to and from school in his Cadillac felt familiar to Nicole, but their friends and teachers saw Mr. Thomas Chapman and his big fancy car in another light. She recognized how some people looked at her and her sister differently because of who her mother was, but it never affected them.

Today, she understands the magnitude of what all that meant for her mom to have touched the lives of so many people worldwide are inspiring. Connecting through music is like a blind universe full of love in its purest form. This was proven to Nicole early on, that anyone of us can touch lives in monumental ways if we do the work.

Tommy did his work servicing people all over the United States. He enjoyed it, and, so far as Nicole knew, no amount of weed smoking ever interfered with his services. The twins were never late for school. It only took a few minutes to get to school from their home, enough time for Tommy to take a few hits on his joint.

They attended Emerson Elementary School, which is still located at 18240 Huntington Street in Detroit, Michigan. The girls had a decent day at school that day. Nothing specific that would be interesting to mention. Nicole remembers feeling normal basically. They were excited about it being Friday because they had family sleepovers most weekends. They also hung out over Grandma Lurlee's, Aunt Max's, or Aunt Pat's home on the weekends. Nicole loved being with her family. She and her cousins were all tight while they were young. They were together always, got along great, and loved one another.

The Ballard family shared genuine love amongst one another. Florence did a lot for her family before having her daughters. Florence's family was also there for her when things weren't so much like the times of success that Nicole heard so much about. Florence shared with her family, even when things were slow, and the money was low. They all went through the before, the during, and the after together wholeheartedly with full support. This was a learned behavior, passed down to the children. The Ballard family would not have had it any other way.

Once the school bell rang and the teachers released the students, Nicole and Michelle ran to the car. They could not wait to get home. Nicole always missed her mom while she was away from her. Tommy was always outside, waiting for his twins when they stepped outside those school doors. Nicole appreciated her dad for treating them so special and precious, which outweighed the unfavorable times. Nicole thinks back on how cool her dad Tommy was.

The car rides together were times with her daddy that she never knew would be moments treasured one day. He was a quiet man, too. As much as he loved music, he never tried being a singer until James Brown's song, "Soul Power," came on. Tommy would sing, "I got soul, and I'm super bad!" Nicole was filled with joy telling this story, describing every detail as if she was envisioning it happening again. It's funnier to her now than it was then, because her father was so serious all the time; it was nice to see him loosen up occasionally.

They were finally in the car and on their way home. Nicole remembers being so anxious to get home that day. She could not wait to find out what their day was going to be like. She always got that information from her mommy. As soon as the wheels stopped rolling, Nicole and Michelle jumped out of the car before their dad could park the car good. They ran to the door and rushed inside, dropping their boots and coats right on the floor of the entryway. Tommy walked in saying, "Mimi (his nickname for Michelle) …Nikki! (his nickname for Nicole) Come to pick y'all stuff up right now!" He was a serious man, not to be mistaken for being mean. Florence gathered the girls' things before they could and put them up for them, but not without reminding them that they should know better.

Florence was a sterner parent than Tommy, but they were a team when it came to teaching their daughters respect, discipline, responsibility, and obedience. Tommy and Florence worked diligently to prepare their daughters for the life ahead, outside the doors of their comfortable home with mom and dad.

A Fishy Tale

Florence told her twin daughters that she had a big surprise for them. They were excited and anxious to find out what was to come. Within thirty minutes of the girls getting home, Florence had gathered the girls and took them to a pet store. Nicole does not remember the name of the pet store, but she does remember the pet store being on Dexter Avenue near the Davison Street area, while she was confident that it was on Dexter Avenue on the Northeast side of Detroit. When they went inside, Florence told them to pick a fish! Nicole and Michelle were so excited. It was their big surprise, after all. They wanted a fish like Arnold (Gary Coleman) had on the television show, *Different Strokes*. Arnold's fish was a Black Moor Goldfish, and his name was Abraham.

The girls didn't want a blackfish once they saw the colorful ones. The salesman informed Florence of everything needed, and she bought it all. They left feeling so excited. The salesman helped them get everything packed up in the trunk properly. They put the

Goldfish upfront with Florence. Nicole was so happy that her mom did not forget that they wanted pet fish. The fish was the only thing Nicole could think of that she did not get from her Christmas list.

She remembers being so anxious to get home, smiling, laughing, and singing songs playing on the radio with her mom and sisters in the car. They made it one block away from the pet store when, all of a sudden, a lady was standing in front of their car, screaming, "Hey Florence Ballard, I love you!" Florence rolled her window down, leaned her head out of the window, and yelled, "I love you too, now get the hell out of my way!" Nicole didn't remember if it was a red light or a stop sign, but she took too long getting out of her mom's way; she knew that much. She watched the lady finish crossing the street while her mom laughed as she made her turn. It was a fun time that Nicole will always remember.

Tommy was still home when the girls and Florence returned from the pet store with everything. It was still early afternoon. The girls were anxious to get inside to show their dad what their mom had bought them. They entered the house boldly, demanding Tommy's immediate attention. The girls took off their coats and boots while their dad went outside to help their mom. Nicole and Michelle watched their parents bring everything inside from the car.

The girls were at full attention while Tommy initiated the ensemble of the newest family members living quarters. The girls would assist with adding the essentials to the fish tank at random with their father. Tommy was doing a splendid job setting it all up by putting all the rocks and statues in the bottom of the tank, while the goldfish swam around in a clear plastic bag filled with water. Tommy began filling the fish tank with water while Florence was nearly done cooking dinner. Nicole remembers having cabbage, because it made her think about the bunny rabbits they saw eating lettuce at the pet shop. Nicole and Michelle laughed about it at the dinner table. They were acting like they were rabbits eating lettuce. By the way, Florence loved cabbage. It was a favorite of hers.

FLORENCE

Tommy finished setting up the fish tank, but he left the fish in their bags. He told his daughters that they would put them in the tank after they ate. Florence fixed everyone's plates. Tommy reminded the twins that they were pet owners, with responsibilities. . The rules and punishments were also discussed.

They were just about finished eating when the doorbell rang. Florence answered the door, and in came Florence's mom and sisters, Lynn and Pat. The twins hurried out of the kitchen to see their grandmother and aunts. Nicole tightly hugged her grandmother. The moment Nicole and Michelle finished getting their hugs from their grandmother and aunts, their dad came into the front room with baby Lisa. Tommy spoke to everyone and hugged his mother-in-law, Lurlee Ballard. She took Lisa from him and started talking and kissing on her.

It was assumed that Florence had already told her mother about the pet fish because Nicole heard her grandmother say, "We came to see your fish." Tommy looked at the girls as they lit up. They all simultaneously made their way to the fish tank, gathered to release the pet fish into their new home. Nicole wanted to introduce their fish to the family.

Florence's sister Lynn asked the girls if they had given their new pet a name yet. They told her yes, and went on to explain which one belongs to whom. "Mine is MoMo, Michelle is BoBo," Nicole yelled. Everybody laughed. The name came from the way their mouths and lips moved when they grab their food. It looked like they were saying Momo and Bobo. The goldfish were the girl's fraternal sister-brother twins. Nicole's fish Bobo had a black spot by his tail. Michelle's fish Momo was a darling little golden girl with dark orange spots around her eyes. Momo was wearing a waterproof eye shadow, explained Nicole.

Their grandmother and aunts stayed a little while before leaving. Once they were gone, Florence went back into the kitchen, singing and sipping on a can of Budweiser beer, which was her favorite. She didn't drink any other brand of beer. She drank beer regularly, and liquor occasionally. Florence was in her zone while cleaning up and preparing supper. She would always sing during her clean up time.

The girls spent more time watching their fish with their daddy. Michelle asked her daddy if they could feed their goldfish now. He told them, "Yes." He picked them up one at a time to let them feed their pet fish. The girls loved watching the fish come to the top to get the smelly floating flakes they ate. Nicole remembers asking her dad why the fish food smelled so funny, but didn't remember his answer. After feeding the fish, the girls played in their bedroom for a while.

The day dwindled down into the evening hours. Florence gathered her family for dinner, which would unknowingly be their final meal together. This would be Florence's last time making spaghetti, which was her specialty, and the girls' favorite. Nicole wonders if her mother Florence loved eating spaghetti too, or just loved making it for them because they didn't get a chance to miss it, for as much as Nicole could recall, Nicole did notice her mom and dad acting a little distant during dinner time. It wasn't alarming, though, so this time, she didn't stay focused on it, maybe because she didn't want to waste another second from getting back to her new pet. Whatever the case was, the girl's bedtime was approaching, and it was time to take a bath.

Florence gave the girls a snack and allowed them to play a little before bed. Maybe thirty minutes passed before Florence came to say goodnight, when the girls asked if they could feed their fish first. Tommy took the girls to feed their fish so their mom could finally tuck them in with a kiss goodnight. Their regular daily routine carried on without a hiccup, but their night would be a different story.

Smell the Smoke – Feel the Burn

This particular night was unusually relaxing for Nicole. She explained that she's usually a light sleeper. Almost any sound could interrupt her sleep. She was having something like a Calgon, take-me-away-moment in bed. It could have been merely a combination of being tired, bathed, and fed in a comfortable, happy, loving atmosphere that contributed to a comfy, peaceful sleep. The sad part is that it only lasted a few short hours.

Suddenly, Nicole woke up to a thump and conflicting commotion. It took a second or two for her to wake up. The next thing she remembers is feeling like her mommy needed her, but still not knowing what was happening. She jumped out of her bed, stumbling from her legs, and getting caught in the covers. She caught herself from falling, but never stopped her mission for one second. She felt the urgency. She could hear better the closer she got to the situation. She remembers hearing a bunch of fussing, struggling, and muffled tones.

Nicole felt that she couldn't arrive soon enough. She ran down the stairs so fast that she now thinks her feet didn't touch each step. Her heart was beating out of her seven-year-old chest so hard that she believes it beat her down the stairs. The noise led her to the kitchen, where she saw her parents on the floor involved a full-on fight. She chose not to share every detail of the fight, because it was the most violent physical altercation she had ever witnessed between her parents.

Although this was not their first fight, it was the last. At that moment, Nicole remembers the beating in her chest so strong and loud from fear of the monster—her dad. She had never felt so angry before. Nicole screamed, "Stop!" She repeated herself over and over, but it was like they didn't hear her. She grew tired of yelling and began sobbing desperately for her mother's rescue.

Her parents suddenly became aware of the scene they had created and witnessed their hopeless uncontrollable actions. She will never forget the look on her father's face when he did what he did to her mom, realizing his daughter was watching him. Tommy and Florence calmed down suddenly. She heard her parents mumble some choice words at one another, then separate upon their rising from the kitchen floor. Tommy was up first, angrily storming out the door. She couldn't look her dad in the face. All she could do was run to her mom and help her up. They hugged as they walked over to the table where Florence sat to compose herself.

Florence cried with her daughter. No mother wants to experience their children witnessing their parents being violent with one another. This made Nicole feel rage toward her dad. She wanted to kill him one day when she was older, for hurting her mother. She hated him for this. Nicole was left with the worst feeling ever that night. Nicole was glad the fight was over, and that her dad was gone.

She held onto her mommy tightly, sobbing. Florence held her daughter, asking her not to cry, telling her that everything will be okay. She wanted her daughter to believe this, but it just was not that simple. It was all comforting to Nicole, and she tried to believe what her mother was saying to her, but by the time her mom put her back to bed and tucked her in, doubt became prevalent.

Does Time Heal All Wounds?

No one claimed that Florence was an angel. In fact, it's been said by her closest loved ones that Florence was very verbal, and not afraid to fight. Florence may have even thrown the first blow. She was not a mundane woman by any shape or form. Still, with Nicole not knowing all the details of her parent's unfortunate battles, not much of it matters when a child witnesses someone hurting their mom. Her dad Tommy was one of the main people hurting her mom repeatedly, and that's how Nicole saw it.

It was hard for her to watch, much harder living with it. Sometimes, Nicole wished she didn't see so much of the abuse between her parents, because now she can't unsee it. All she could think about was how much her mother needed her at that time. Nicole thought her mom needed her, but later realized it was, in fact, she who needed her mommy. She needed so desperately for her mother to be all right, and to know that her mom was safe and well-protected. Nicole was concerned about her mom's wellbeing so much that she tried to fix what she thought she could, while getting assistance from other family members to help her mom with what Nicole felt she couldn't resolve on her own. Nicole wanted to protect her mother's heart, if you can understand that, but she didn't know how. She wasn't big enough to protect her physically, so she focused on trying to heal her heart from all the pain that had been seemingly consuming her and affecting her progress in life.

Today, when Nicole looks back on this incident, she wonders if something went wrong on or around Valentine's Day. She wonders if this last fight had anything to do with a Valentine's Day dismay. This could have fueled the beginning of her parents' ending. She pondered over what could have gone so wrong that it carried over to February 20th. It wasn't odd for a disagreement to extend over a week. She had witnessed situations stretch out longer than that after an argument.

Nicole saw her dad as a very jealous man who always accused her mom of seeing someone else. Nicole has witnessed her parents argue over other men and how her mom handled the encounters a few times. Tommy had issues with Florence being too friendly with her male counterparts. She couldn't be too kind, or it would signal deceit to Tommy. Florence had a smile that proved to be a gift and a curse. A beautiful gift to the world, but a curse for her husband Tommy's ego.

It's never been confirmed if Florence was ever guilty of his assumptions. Nothing admitted by Florence that anyone knows of, or have mentioned, ever verified it. There is an interview with Otis Williams, the founding member of Motown's legendary male soulful singing group, The Temptations, where he claimed to have had an affair with Florence in 1962, during the Motown Revue Tour. Being a married man at the time, Otis only partook in this affair for the duration of that particular tour.

Florence was on this tour as a temporary replacement for The Marvelettes vocal member Wanda Young, while she was out on maternity leave. Tommy must have heard about this rumor and quite possibly had known it to be true. This would explain Tommy's shifting comfort level when Florence would spend time around her Motown family, specifically The Temptations, even though it had been five years since Mr. Williams and Florence had their rumored affair (also being before Tommy and Florence's time together).

The odd behavior that was displayed from Tommy was considered jealousy, which could have been misjudged for fear. Tommy may have felt fear of losing his beloved wife, Florence, to one of the established artists to whom he may have felt inferior. It was not a matter of Tommy wanting any of their positions, because it was evident that Tommy was happy with the work he did. The gatherings became uncomfortable for Tommy and Florence both, for different reasons. This would give a reason as to why Florence's behavior towards her fellow Motown family members changed when she and Tommy would be in their company together. Florence became distant and secluded.

FLORENCE

Florence was still unsettled with her career turnout after the failed success of being signed to ABC Records in New York immediately after leaving Motown. The plan she left with did not turn out favorable for her. Many people believed in her and her solo career. After all, many Supremes fans felt that Florence was the group's true lead and voice. Florence and her husband, Tommy, decided to build a studio in their home and try for this solo career again. With all the love and support Florence had, anyone would have easily assumed that her solo career would work out for sure this time.

Once Florence completed her in-house music studio, she dove back into music so heavily; it brought joy back into her life. Florence and Tommy believed that they would save money this time by recording themselves in their own studio lab. Studio time can get pricey.

Florence found hope again in music and the magic that it brings. They started having parties that brought Motown's finest out. Florence shared her joy of recording with all of her fellow Motown music family that would come. They were able to collaborate on songs and critique one another, helping with the production and engineering of the music they were creating. It was almost as if everyone automatically knew Florence and Tommy's situation, as well as what was to be expected of them during their visits. Tommy got along with everyone. Not one of them had a personal vendetta against him, besides those who felt Tommy was ridiculous and unreasonable at times, to Florence's defense. The main defenders would include Florence's lovely overprotective sisters, and a few others closest to them.

Nevertheless, the love amongst them all remained with much respect eventually gained. Many good times came with the gatherings, but Florence loved to be alone in her studio and zone out to hers or other artists' music. This carried on for a while, before things just kind of slowed down naturally. Florence became pregnant again with her last baby girl, Lisa. Tommy and Florence were having marital issues. Trust was not a strong suit for them, which kept the dysfunction in their relationship alive with a healthy appetite. Nicole did have a comfortable, peaceful sleep knowing that her dad was gone and not home to hurt her mom anymore, for now.

Dr. Jekyll, What Are You Hiding?

When Nicole woke up again, it was morning. She smelled breakfast cooking downstairs and music playing. She got up and found her mom in the kitchen in good spirits singing Al Green, "Love and Happiness" while scrambling eggs. Everything appeared to be okay even though she knew better. It was pleasing to see her mom cheerful after being in an unhappy space just a few hours earlier.

The girls ate, dressed, and then Florence took them to visit with her mother, Lurlee. The ride there was unusually quiet. Everything switched. It was such a sad ride that Nicole despaired even more. Florence was holding up well before they left, but now she appeared sunken and broken . It was like a Dr. Jekyll and Mr. Hyde moment which confirmed things were not okay. Nicole watched her mom the whole ride. She saw her make up smear and her eyeliner running down her face with tears. She saw her trying to cover up bruises on her leg as well. It was sad and pitiful at this moment because Nicole knew that her mom was still hiding the truth. Nicole just wanted her mommy to be happy, but she didn't know how to make that happen.

She couldn't wait to arrive at her grandma's house, hoping and thinking maybe that would cheer her up, but in the back of her mind, she knew it wouldn't turn out that way. Everything was always Tommy's fault, so she knew they would be angry, seeing Florence hurt physically and mentally. Florence had to deal with her family harboring feelings of resentment towards her husband, Tommy. Her family did not feel Tommy was worthy of Florence, mostly because of his blatant abuse toward her. They wouldn't have to wait much longer to find out how their attitudes toward Tommy would be concerning this altercation between Florence and him.

Florence and her daughters finally made it to her mother's house, but no bolting to the door this visit. The twins took time to help their mommy get Lisa and her things instead. Grandma Lurlee greeted them at the door, hugging and kissing them as they walked in. She asked if anyone was hungry. She always had something ready to eat. We didn't have much of an appetite after eating breakfast already. Florence sat in the living room, talking with her mom and baby sister Lynn. Children were not allowed to sit with the adults when they were talking. The kids would be instructed to play outside or in the basement during their talks. They knew she was angry, and venting. They were tired of Florence and Tommy fussing and fighting. Florence would go to her mom's house to vent and release anger when she and Tommy would be troubled. Nicole, being overly concerned for her mom, never hesitated to pop up here and there hearing bits and pieces of their conversation. Nicole was doing simple wellness checks on her mom just to see if she was cheering up any.

During one of her pop-ups, she heard her mom tell her grandmother Lurlee that, if something happened to her, to take them into your custody. "Them" being her daughters. Nicole felt then, as she still does today, that her mother was speaking from hurt and anger, although there could have been some reasoning behind it that Nicole may not have been privy to for many reasons. She knew her mom loved her dad, even though she did not trust him. She was only reactive to this judgment when he performed in the worst ways. It was all love otherwise, something like a happy, loving family, one to be proud of. But this last altercation between Florence and Tommy was probably the most damming, with the most remarkable effects.

    Florence seemed unbalanced since leaving home. Her mental state was impaired to the extent that it made her seven-year-old daughter Nicole aware. It was evident that Florence was hurt and fed up, but this time she wore her pain on her sleeve, which she displayed in a self-destructive way. Things did calm down with Florence, her sisters, and their mom Lurlee after starting with so much tension. They proceeded with their conversation cautiously, while periodically lending whispers amongst one another. This carried on for a short time before the ladies relaxed their tones enough to comfort Florence's daughter Nicole's curiosity. This moment allowed Nicole to take this opportunity to take a seat on the sofa near them. She sat there watching television and eavesdropping on what was left of their exclusive conversation.

    Nicole noticed her mom getting ice and eating it out of a cup. This puzzled Nicole to see her mom try to heal herself by eating ice. It turned out to be much more than any of them could have imagined. The cause of her discomfort and confusion while she ate ice never came to a clear understanding.

    Nicole's grandmother Lurlee asked her daughter Florence, "Why do you keep getting ice to eat?" Florence replied, "I'm hot and can't cool down no matter what I do." The ice gave her temporary relief but was more effective than a cold drink, which was assumed because she repeatedly chose ice over ice-cold beverages. Florence's mother and sister Lynn looked bothered by her current condition and mental state. It was confusing to them, but it did not seem as serious then as it became later.

Getting medical attention was mentioned to Florence, but not in a forceful way. You would think the person dealing with the illness would know what is best for themselves. The reality is that sometimes we don't seek medical attention when we should; instead, we procrastinate, thinking we will get better on our own. Other times, we wait until it's too late, allowing the illness to worsen over time. Once the condition worsens, it can cause trauma and shock to your body's system and organs, triggering more issues, which can prove to be fatal.

The ride home from her grandmother's house wasn't any better. Nicole sat in the front seat, watching her try to hide the bruising on her leg a few times. They rode home quietly, listening to the radio. Nicole didn't know what to expect when they got home. She was hoping her dad wasn't there first and foremost. She thought if her dad stayed gone for a while, it might have given her mommy a chance to get herself together and maybe live free and happy for a change. When they made it home, Nicole noticed that her dad was not there. That relaxed her mind to some degree. Florence asked the girls to go upstairs to their room and play. It was apparent to Nicole that Florence was trying to have some time to herself, but she didn't want to leave her mother's side.

Nicole went upstairs with her sisters to play and get out of her mom's way so she can have a moment to herself. They carried on without worrying about anything serious. The girls were typically good, respectful and obedient girls. Besides the typical sisterly squabbles here and there, these sisters got along well. The house was calm, and everyone felt safe for the time being. Time was passing in an unforgettable time warp that would haunt them forever.

Florence was home getting a quick meal together while her daughters entertained themselves upstairs. Nothing more than a few yells from Florence upstairs to ask the girls to quiet down, or to answer a question from the girls yelling down to her. This wouldn't happen much. The girls knew when it was time to behave and give their mommy a break. They didn't interrupt their mother's peace much, if at all most times. When dysfunction was relevant, and the girls were concerned for their mom's wellbeing, happiness is when they would appear repeatedly. Overly-anxious is how Nicole described the way she remembers herself feeling.

Nicole could hear her mom downstairs on the phone, talking to her mother, Lurlee. She couldn't remember any specifics about the conversation besides the fact that her mommy Florence was still angry with her dad, as was she. She could hear her mother moving about the house all over the place, cussing about the things she was unhappy with her life to her mom on the phone. Florence being upset, was expected and didn't raise any eyebrows. As long as Nicole didn't hear her father walking through the door, she didn't worry too much about her mommy while she played with her sisters.

Meanwhile, Florence was well into her hurt. There was heavy disappointment attached this time. She called for the girls to come down to eat. They ate a quick meal then had some playtime in the bathtub. Florence cleaned up and got the girls ready for bed. The girls went back upstairs with snacks this time. Nicole was beginning to worry about her mom again.

The girls would go downstairs to use the bathroom and look at their pet fish Momo and Bobo, before going back upstairs. Nicole began to worry about her mother a little more. It was a different kind of hurt in her mommy's tone, and eyes that she remembers sadly. She felt anxious to see about her mother. Nicole stayed upstairs long enough to get her sisters situated basically, before making her way back downstairs to her mom.

This long day finally settled into a confused but acceptable evening. Nicole returned to her mom by helping her clean up. She brought down all the trash from the snacks she and her sisters had upstairs. She then proceeded to assist her mom. Nicole could tell that her mommy had at least one or two beers while they were upstairs. Florence usually let Nicole get away with hanging around with her when she was more relaxed. Nicole saw her mom make a drink instead of opening a beer, this time opening up a liquor bottle. Nicole can't remember the type of liquor or what she mixed it with in her cup. She does remember her mom would mix a little bit of liquor in her coffee, but that didn't happen much that Nicole could attest to. Florence usually chose a Budweiser beer over any drink.

All the cleanup was done, so Nicole sat quietly, watching her mother as she sipped on her drink and smoked a cigarette. Nicole knew her mom would be headed to the basement soon. It was her special place to go, no matter her mood. Nicole loved watching her mom sing. She was her number one fan. Florence kept singing and humming a tune like she was trying to practice or remember a song she wrote. This was normal for Florence, as she was desperately working on her new solo work. She was always singing "People" by Barbara Streisand, her favorite song to sing to warm up. Nicole followed her mom downstairs to the basement studio but stopped and sat on the steps, as she usually did. Doing more than that could cause her mom to ask her to go upstairs and go to bed. As a child, Nicole learned early how to stick around without getting sent away or in trouble by sitting still and being quiet.

Once they were in position downstairs, there was a slight pause in the song. As Nicole looked on, she saw her mommy take a pill or two, then returned to singing as if nothing happened. Florence did take prescription medicine, making this nothing to be alarmed about. If anything, it would have been the drinking that was cause for alarming concern. Nicole continued watching her mom sing, drink, and smoke cigarettes for the next twenty minutes or so until she fell asleep on the step. Florence carried her daughter to her room and put her in bed. Nicole recalls everything going downhill from there.

SUPREME EXIT

Stop the Clock

  The night was calm and quiet, with a cinch of sadness overcasting the Chapman household. The girls were all in bed now resting peacefully, except for Nicole. She was always the last to fall asleep. Eventually, feeling defeated, she started dozing off. Echoes of a determined Florence singing downstairs were the last sounds Nicole remembers hearing before drifting off into a deep sleep. A deep comfortable sleep, as she recalls it, one that she remembers feeling so great that she can never forget the way it was disrupted.

  Fights between Florence and Tommy were not uncommon inside the Chapman household. It somewhat felt normal, but the fact that this one cycle of incidents, at that moment time proved to be the end-all for everyone making every dimension of it unforgettable. The devastation caused these scenes to replay in Nicole's mind regularly from then on throughout her lifetime. Nicole felt like someone came to steal her joy like a thief in the night. This would be the last time that Nicole would ever have such a peaceful sleep in a long time.

Sleeping beauty's comfort was successfully stolen by that evil thief while abruptly interrupting her rest.

She doesn't know what woke her up; she just remembers jumping up out of her bed and getting downstairs quickly. When she reached the bottom step, she could see her mom sitting in the dining room in a chair with her arms and head loosely sprawled across the table.

She wasn't sitting up. She was slumped, her arms stretched along the table, barely holding her head upright. The unnatural disposition of her legs was a concerning site. Nicole was frantic when she asked her mommy if she was okay. Florence tried to respond, but her words didn't come out. Nicole approached her mother while trying to assess this situation, making Nicole more saddened by the minute. Florence tried to tell Nicole to go back upstairs by gesturing her hand toward the stairway. Nicole knew her mother was trying to protect her from seeing too much. A typical reaction from a concerned and protective parent trying, to minimize the effects of family dysfunction.

Nicole understood her mother's intention as she paused to think about it for a second. Because Nicole knew something was seriously wrong, she decided to stay and probe into her mother's situation more. Her mother's energy seemed depleted by her gesture wave to Nicole. Her arm barely rose from the table. No way am I turning away now, was Nicole's instant thought. She was nervous approaching her mom now, because she didn't understand what was happening and didn't know what to do.

Florence didn't want Nicole to see her in this state, but it was too late. Florence tried to turn away from Nicole by the time she reached her. Nicole's fear deepened once she saw her face. There was white stuff (known as foam) on her face and mouth. Now, this is scary for a seven-year-old child to witness, but she knew enough to know that this was so bad that it might be too much for her to handle alone. The helplessness Nicole felt brought on a flow of tears. She was unable to stop the tears from falling.

She did not want to cry. She wanted her mommy to be able to attest to her strength in this unexpected test of time. Nicole thought if she could show her mommy that she can remain calm and assist with caring for her now, Florence would trust her daughter's mature abilities to allow her to be more involved and informed. That was not the case here, and time was passing with no progress. Nicole was beginning to give in to her enormous amount of fear when she found herself bawling inconsolably. She cried so hard that her sisters must have heard her.

The sound of someone coming downstairs commanded Nicole's attention. It was her sisters. She met up with them near the bottom of the steps, stopping them from coming down. Nicole knew her mother did not want her daughters to see her in this state, so she yelled for them to go back up. She told them that she would be back up there in a minute. Michelle and Lisa went back up without incident.

Nicole knew that something had to happen now. She called Motown and left a message for her dad to come home. She then called her grandmother and Aunt Lynn. She told Lynn that mommy couldn't walk or talk, and white stuff was on her mouth. Lynn was panicking because Nicole was crying, and Florence couldn't speak. Lynn tried talking to Florence on the phone, but she couldn't respond and seemed bothered, like she wanted to be left alone unless you could help her. Nicole put the phone back to her ear and told her Aunt Lynn that she couldn't leave her mom's side, but she was emotionally traumatized seeing her mom like this. She knew her mom was not okay in the worst way.

This was something Nicole had never witnessed. Nicole would try to lift her mom and sit her upright, but Florence kept dropping her head and going limp. She tried to talk to Nicole, but the sudden strike in communication was frustrating. It was difficult and exhausting for her to articulate. Nicole could not understand how her mom was just fine a few hours ago, now all of a sudden, she couldn't walk or talk.

Nicole explained all of this to her Aunt Lynn. Her grandmother Lurlee was near Lynn, listening all along. She took the phone from Lynn and asked if Nicole talked to her dad. She told her grandmother that she did call, and she left a message. Her grandmother said to her that she was doing a good job. She told Nicole to put the phone to Florence's ear so that she could speak to her. Grandmother Lurlee talked to her daughter, telling her that everything would be okay, and they will be there with her as soon as they could get there. Nicole returned to the phone, where her grandmother was waiting on the other end. She told Nicole to go get a towel, wet it, and lay it across her mom's forehead. She remembered her daughter being unable to cool her body temperature down from being so hot just one day before visiting her house. If only that were all they needed to fix her daughter. Nicole got the wet towel and placed it across her mom's forehead. It did seem to soothe her mom, so she continued doing it. Her Aunt Lynn returned to the phone and told Nicole that she would call her back after she called her dad.

Lynn called Motown looking for Tommy as well. Tommy returned Lynn's call within minutes. Lynn asked him to pick her up so she could see about her sister too. Tommy made it to pick Lynn up, then urgently headed to Florence. Nicole was still holding up well caring for her mom. She brought ice and water to her mommy, trying to do anything to aid in her healing. Florence would appear irritated during her care from her daughter at times. Florence thought that she could handle herself. She tried moving around on her own, but it just wasn't happening. Her legs were like noodles. Florence noticeably realized her sudden handicap.

The look of helplessness on her mother's face was heartbreaking to Nicole. She hugged her mom and told her, "You're going to be okay and help is on the way." It was a moment easily described as "terrifusing," terrifying and confusing at the same time. Florence was fine a few hours ago, now all of a sudden, her breath was short, and her strength was gone.

Nicole tried everything she could think of and what she was told to do, praying that any of it would make her mommy better, but nothing soothed her. She couldn't get words outright; her breath was short, and her strength was gone. Nicole couldn't make out what her mom was trying to say to her, except when she would try to send her back upstairs with her sisters. She didn't know what was happening to her mom, and it frightened her terribly.

Nicole stayed by her mom's side. She couldn't leave her. Time had elapsed, but she did not have to go at it alone much longer because her dad and aunt were entering the front door. Nicole was relieved but remained alert and present, ready to assist her father and aunt in any way necessary. Nicole felt in her mind that an adult would be able to assess her mother's condition better, and possibly fix her.

Tommy and Lynn went straight to Florence asking all types of questions, but once again, Florence could not speak coherently. She tried to respond to everyone; it just wouldn't come outright. Lynn decided to move her sister Florence from the chair to a more comfortable spot. Lynn picked her sister up and sat her on the sofa a few feet away from the dining room table Florence was sitting at when Lynn got there.

Lynn just took charge out of nowhere, with no hesitation. They had no idea what Lynn was about to do until it was done. It was a struggle going at it alone, but Lynn managed to move her big sister promptly and safely. Once Lynn got Florence situated on the sofa, she fired up her investigation with more questions. She asked Nicole a series of questions like, "Did she have something to drink, what did she drink, did she eat or take anything?" Nicole answered her dad and her Aunt Lynn's questions as well as she could, with great hope that her answers would help her mom. They were asking questions randomly, rapidly, and repeatedly. It was confusing and frustrating because nobody knew what to do honestly, besides calling an ambulance for immediate medical and professional assistance.

The adults felt this was much different than the effects of consuming too much alcohol. They believed Florence's unfathomable condition had to do with more than a night of binge drinking. Lynn wanted to know everything that her niece could remember. Tommy went looking for medications while they waited for the ambulance to arrive.

Tommy approached Nicole with a few bottles that he found on the bedroom dresser, since Nicole had mentioned seeing her mom take one or two pills. Tommy asked his daughter if she knew which pill or pills her mom took, but Nicole had no idea what medication her mother took. Tommy also showed Florence the bottles one by one, and asked her if it was what she took or not. They reported all they knew to the emergency team.

Florence did try to answer their questions a few times, but one must wonder if maybe some of the answers Florence gave were even considered due to her assumed state of being inebriated and or delirious. Tommy was so confused and concerned as he watched the emergency team work on his wife. Nicole had never really seen her dad look like he was unsure or didn't have a handle on things like this night. While everyone found themselves in total focus on Florence, she uttered to her daughter Nicole, "You're in charge!" Something she had instructed Nicole before.

The paramedics began to pack up and secure Florence as they carried her out on the stretcher, with Tommy following behind. Lynn stayed behind to situate her nieces while Tommy accompanied his wife to the hospital in the back of the ambulance. It finally felt like things were on the road to getting better. For sure, this was nothing a doctor couldn't fix. It did not seem as bad as it turned out right then. In maybe five minutes, the ambulance arrived, assessed Florence, and left. The entire ordeal seemed longer than it was because through it all, Florence was gone in an instant.

Tick Tock

Nicole's Aunt Pat made it over to Florence's house after the ambulance left. Lynn was inside gathering her thoughts, then called her mother to inform her of Florence's condition, providing updates. Mrs. Lurlee was satisfied with the information her daughter Lynn provided about Florence, before hanging up the phone. She waited patiently for her daughters Lynn and Pat to come home with her granddaughters. Lynn went upstairs to wake the girls up and get them dressed to go home with her for the night.

By the time Lynn had the girls together and ready to go, the ambulance had arrived at Mount Carmel Hospital on McNichols, which is historically known as Six Mile Road at Outer Drive, on the Northwest side of Detroit. This emergency care facility was closest to Florence's home, taking the ambulance only a few minutes to get her there.

Florence's sisters Pat and Max, along with Max's son Chris met Florence and Tommy at the hospital soon after they arrived. Everyone felt optimistic about Florence's recovery as they took control and organized in-home care for her upon her discharge. A few of Florence's family members went to her home to prepare her a clean and comfortable place to recover. No one knew Florence better than her family, which made it easy for them to know how to satisfy her every want and need. Florence's family was concerned and intensely angry. Because Florence was not communicating effectively, no one knew the factual information dealing with the intimate details of what caused Florence's current situation.

It had only been one day ago that Florence and Tommy were at odds and physically abusive to one another. One can only wonder if Tommy played any part in Florence's demise. Florence could not answer the questions her family had for her at that time. This delay in clarification was acceptable due to the natural thought that they would get to discuss all of their concerns and get to the bottom of what happened the moment Florence was able to communicate. That was somewhat comforting for the moment.

Meanwhile, there was reserved suspicion, which caused misunderstood tension. Everyone knew to place their feelings aside for now. Staying focused on Florence was their primary concern. Regular reports were made to Florence's mother, Lurlee, keeping her updated on her daughters' condition. The word was spreading throughout the family very quickly. Everyone who cared most was aware and concerned. It was said that she was doing better and seemed to be in good spirits before they left her side in the hospital. Florence needed to get some rest. Everyone felt a sigh of relief that now the healing process begins. They all believed that Florence was going to be alright.

Nicole, Michelle, and Lisa made it to their grandmother Lurlee's house with Lynn. The girls were marched right into their aunt's bedroom to get settled in and relax. All Nicole could think about was her mommy getting better and coming home soon. Nicole tried to sleep, but she doesn't remember if she ever fell asleep. She remembers lying on her back, looking up at the ceiling, talking to God. She prayed for her parents often but her mother most. Maybe a bit much for a child Nicole's age. So much concern and responsibility coming from a child to harbor. Nicole eavesdropped on every phone call and conversation, waiting on the magic words that her mom was fine and on her way home.

Most of the calls came from family members asking what happened to Florence and for updates on her condition. Mrs. Lurlee told someone that Tommy called her and said the doctor explained that Florence was doing better and would be fine. It felt promising to the family, who expected a quick recovery.

Nicole finally closed her eyes and got some rest. Soon after, the phone rang, waking Nicole up again. She heard her grandmother answer the call. The conversation was quick and disturbing. Her dad Tommy was on the line, informing his mother-in-law that the doctor had notified him that Florence's condition had worsened, and he needed to return to the hospital immediately. This news was alarming to Lurlee as can be imagined.

The family waited anxiously to hear back from Tommy. Meanwhile, Florence's mother and sister Lynn discussed their concerns, but were clueless and confused. This incident was beginning to appear a lot more severe than they had initially assumed it to be.

Their worries intensified. Nicole remembered hearing her aunt and grandmother discussing their concerns with one another, and all they could say was, "I don't know," a number of times because there were so many unanswered questions. It was an unsure, scary, and confusing moment. Nicole was nervous but quiet and still. She didn't know how to feel. She wanted to believe that everything would be okay, just like she told her mom, Florence. No one thought this would be the end of Florence Ballard Chapman's life. Her final moment here on earth was a compelling thought that no one seemed to visit or invite into their mind.

Nicole was afraid that her mother could die because of how ill she was, but once the ambulance came and Florence made it to the hospital, she was sure that the doctors were going to fix her mommy and send her home with a to-do list and everything would go back to the way it was. Maybe the doctor would find that Florence just ate something bad or took the wrong medication that made her sick, although the feeling that things were really bad never left. It was a waiting game that kept everyone on edge. Nicole walked over and asked them if they would take her to see her mommy. They told her they would take her soon after they hear back from her dad.

She felt comforted in knowing before long; she would be seeing her mom again. She went back into the room where her sisters were to lie down. After yawning a few times, Nicole was finally sound asleep. She must have been drained by then and just could not fight it any longer, as it was already the crack of dawn. When she opened her eyes again, it would not take long to change her view on life.

A few hours had gone by before Lurlee saw her granddaughter's bright little faces again. The sun rose, and so did Nicole and the rest of Florence Ballard Chapman's loved ones, but the news was about to break that Florence went to sleep for good. She did not wake up this time.

It was a complete nightmare with a shattering new reality approaching this family. Nicole could not stop worrying about her mom. Before long, she was up because she could not rest anymore. She got up and walked past her grandmother, who sat in the living room with her daughter Lynn, waiting to hear an update on Florence. Lynn went into the kitchen to prepare food for her nieces. Nicole met

FLORENCE

up with her Aunt Lynn in the kitchen. She asked if she's still going to see her mom. Lynn told her that her dad called and that he would be there soon to pick them up. Nicole assumed that her dad would be taking them to visit their mother in the hospital instead of her Aunt Lynn taking them, since they mentioned they were waiting on her dad to arrive. That worked for Nicole, but made her anxious for her father to get there.

Michelle and Lisa also joined Nicole and their Aunt Lynn in the kitchen to eat. Lynn situated her nieces before returning to the living room. After eating a little bit of the food, the girls finished up in the kitchen before they all returned to the living room area. Nicole found a spot on the floor sitting near the sofa where her aunt and grandmother sat, slowly zoning in and out, getting comfortable as she patiently awaited her father's arrival. She sat still thinking and listening while blankly staring at the television. Everyone was watching television, or it was watching them, so Nicole explains. She became more relaxed and noticed that she paid more attention to whatever show was playing on the television set.

The house was calm as everyone sat quietly together watching television when, suddenly, there was an interruption for breaking news. A news reporter came on and said, "Florence Ballard, the former original group member and founder of The Supremes, has died." That was all Nicole remembered hearing before she turned to her Aunt Lynn and screamed, "My mommy died!" Mrs. Lurlee let out a horrible sound of the deepest heartbreak imaginable. Lynn hugged Nicole tight, saying, "I'm sorry, baby. We did not want y'all to find out like this." They all cried together. No one expected this outcome. Lynn and her mother, Lurlee, had received a call from Tommy at least an hour before Nicole and her sisters woke up. It was hard for them to keep their emotions intact so the kids wouldn't be aware. Nicole's grandmother, Lurlee, cried so hard. It was hard to know what hurt her more, losing a daughter or her granddaughters losing a mother. Nicole wrestled with thoughts of why and how her mom died, but she understood that her mother wasn't coming back home, and she would never see her again.

She thought about her sisters, Michelle and Lisa, and how they must be feeling. How she could protect them weighed heavily on her mind for a very long time. She felt she needed to keep herself together and be strong for her sisters. She prayed, "Lord God, please help me be strong for my sisters and make mommy proud." The tears were still falling as she prayed in silence. Florence reportedly died from a coronary thrombosis.

They all were a mess now. No one needed to hide their hurt anymore, although the adults controlled their level of emotions, careful not to upset the girls any more than they were already. That only lasted a short time, since Florence's sisters Maxine and Pat walked through the door dismantled. The pain was piercing them all, as if they all were physically connected. It was the saddest moment of Nicole's life.

Soon after, Tommy arrived to pick up his daughters. He came straight from the hospital. The second Nicole saw her dad, she ran into his arms and said, "Mommy died." Tommy cried, barely holding his head up, saying, "I love you." Seeing Tommy's face looking lost and broken shattered Nicole even more. Tommy grabbed his girls and held them tight. He never said to them that their mom died. It's possible that he couldn't say those words to his daughters. It was hard enough seeing the hurt on their little faces as it was. Everyone hugged Lurlee to console her too. The amount of emotion in that room alone was extremely too much to bear at that moment. Tommy walked over to comfort her mother in law before leaving. They stood and hugged each other.

Tommy packed his daughters up and headed home. Nicole closed her eyes for most of the ride. Tommy and Florence drove the same route, making the scenery and certain landmarks hard for Nicole to look at. Searching for the answers to surviving this devastation in her head, she heard her mommy say, "You're in charge." She had to be strong for her sisters. She could not and would not let her mother down. Then the radio station made an announcement about Florence. Tommy tried to turn the station before much was said, but it was too late. Nicole watched tears stream down her father's face from the rearview mirror. She closed her eyes again and cried solemnly.

Slow Motion

Walking back into the house gave off a weird feeling for them all. The fact that her mom wasn't on the other side of the door, down the hall, in the kitchen, bedroom, bathroom, basement, or anywhere was killing Nicole inside. After clearing her semi-search efforts for her mother, she stopped for a moment and sat on the basement steps where she always sat when she watched her mommy practice singing her songs downstairs in the studio. She could see her mom when she closed her eyes, but her mom was never there when she would open up her eyes again. It hurt her really bad.

The last time Nicole closed her eyes sitting on those steps, she heard a voice say, "Nikki… Nikki." It was not her mom, because it was the voice of a man. It was a little confusing, because she'd just heard her mom's voice calling her name not too long ago. She sat still and quiet as tears continued to fall from her eyes. She needed to hear it again before she moved, and to be certain it was not her mother. Of course, she absolutely wanted it to be her, but then she felt someone touch her on her shoulder.

When she looked up, she saw that it was her dad trying to get her attention. Tommy sat with his daughter Nicole for a minute, holding her and telling her that he loves her over and over again. He told her, "We will be ok." Nicole said, "No we won't, daddy."

He grabbed her so tight, then grouped all of his girls together in the living room to talk. He sat them down to explain where their mother was and that they all would see her body again one last time soon. He added, "She will be dressed up beautifully like when she was a star on stage. Daddy loves y'all and we gone make it through this together." He consoled and comforted them before he tucked them in bed with love, just like their mommy used to. Nicole lied in bed, staring at the walls and ceiling, trying to look through the drywall to see into heaven in the hopes of getting a glimpse of her mother.

Nicole was an emotional wreck, feeling lost just wanting her mommy just as any child in her predicament would. She began to have mixed feelings about her father when she thought about him fighting and hurting her mother. Her dad was so hurt and distraught over her mom's passing; she felt compassion for him, as did many others. It was written all over his face. She never saw her dad cry so much over anything. That made it hard for Nicole to hold a grudge against her dad. She had truly hated him just hours ago, and thought she would be the one to grow up and kill him for hurting her mommy.

After losing her mother so tragically and unexpectedly, it did not make much sense to hold a grudge against the only living parent she had left, who loved her despite all things done and thoughts of others. She felt the love exude from within towards her dad as she rationalizes the fact that he's all she has now, finalizing her decision to let go of the hurt and pain Tommy caused. She forgave her dad at that moment and asked God to forgive her for thinking such evil thoughts upon her father.

For a while, Nicole's last moments at home with her mom replayed in her head every day, all day. She often wondered what could or should she have done to have maybe saved her mother that day. That moment is something that she can still see, hear, smell, and taste. It will live in her forever.

Nicole and Michelle's teachers, Ms. Thomas and Mr. Cunningham, were very kind and patient with them after losing their mother. Florence's passing was national news, and the entire school staff was aware of Nicole and Michelle being the daughters of Florence Ballard. The girls were given extra attention and comfort when it looked like they had difficult moments in class by most, if not all, of their teachers, but mostly by Mr. Cunningham and Ms. Thomas, who went the extra mile for them. This helped them get through the day, and to be able to focus on their schoolwork long enough to complete assignments on time. Nicole and Michelle are thankful to them for taking the time to show a genuine concern that Florence probably appreciates. Nicole needed as much attention as possible from whoever had it to give. All the extra love and attention were necessary as Nicole began to feel increasingly lost without her mom. All the love in the world couldn't replace her mother's love and attention. Florence made her daughter feel special.

The realization kept setting in and would not stop. Constant reminders were everywhere. It was hard for Nicole to be home, but she didn't want to be anywhere else. She just wanted her mom there with her and her sisters. Nicole prayed that her mom would be healed and sent home, which did not happen. That angered Nicole for a while.

As the news on Florence's passing spread, people began to drop things off on the Chapman's doorstep like flowers, cards, letters, and other small things. Some of their neighbors stopped by to offer their condolences, bearing cakes, pies, and other food items for the taking. It was always a warm feeling when people came, but it also made it more real for Nicole each time. All of this made Nicole think about how fans would stop Florence while she would be out with her mom. The fans would ask Florence to sing, and they would tell her how they thought she had a better voice out of all of the Supremes. Fans were serious with their support. You would think they had a real conversation with Florence, giving them much detail to feel comfortable enough to judge in such ways. Florence loved all her fans and gave them the real Florence all the time. No matter how torn she felt inside, she was good at hiding what was going on in her private life.

Before Florence died, her fans were bold enough to show up on her doorstep and knock, or ring the doorbell. Most would stand in the yard and call out her name. Can you imagine hearing strangers at random standing in your yard yelling out your mother's name? It was weird to Nicole, but she saw her mom deal with it with such grace. There were times when she was sad, but would still answer to her fans with a smile. A public figure trying to keep her personal business matters private and separate work from family wasn't easy, but Florence did an excellent job, and was even better at it after leaving Motown.

The Unreachable

The next few days were as hard as anyone could imagine. Nicole experienced being more confused, dazed out, and in shock than she was awake and focused in real-time. She felt robotic and numb while executing chores and such like clockwork. This may be accredited to being rote acts, where the body physically functions on auto mode because of repetition.

Reality would slap her in the face often just to remind her that misery and depression were real. This was when the depression started for Nicole, which is around the time frame anyone would suspect a child her age to feel from the absence of her mother. Nicole concealed it by being more concerned for her sisters and their needs, which she attended to naturally. The responsibility of protecting Michelle and Lisa wasn't Nicole's, but she took it on as if it were so.

She would only allow her depression to take flight when she was alone. She couldn't let her sisters see her down and out, looking hopeless and weak. That would not help her sisters as much as she could help them by inspiring them with strength, courage, and wisdom instead. She constantly consoled her baby sister Lisa, and took more time to supply a mother's love that she would miss dearly one day.

Nicole always did things for Lisa the way Florence did, in hopes of not interrupting the pattern. She knew she could not replace her mom, so she tried to do as much as she could, the way Florence did to try to fill some of the void of not having a mother. In Nicole's mind, she needed to fill her mother's shoes to keep things normal, resembling how things were always done in their home. It worked sometimes, and without noticing, things would just operate smoothly.

FLORENCE

However, other times, it would bring sadness once the natural desires of wanting your mother sneak in. Florence's family were close and overly supportive of one another's grievance. Everyone took a shift to accommodate the needs of the children Florence left behind, and they dedicated themselves entirely, contributing to raising them.

DETROIT FREE PRESS February 28, 1976

The Final Curtain Call

Ready or not, the big day for everyone to say their final goodbyes to the lovely Florence Ballard Chapman had come. This had to be as hard as anyone could imagine. Tommy held it together well enough to manage and appear all set for periods of time until bouts of emotions hit high peaks as he wrestled with the obvious. The sadness was inevitable.

Tommy moved throughout the house while the girls were in their room, gathering themselves and their things. Nicole seized the moment to strengthen her sisters with a few words by telling them that it's okay to be sad but try not to cry because mommy had to go to heaven. This was all that Nicole could think of to say to her sisters. She would remind them of this when Lisa asked for her mommy, or when Michelle cried about missing their mommy.

Lynn made sure that her nieces were well put together for their mother's homegoing service with every attempt to impress. Lynn pressed the girl's dresses and hung them neatly and orderly. Lynn was a great help and did a wonderful job with her nieces. Lynn was on top of it all and did not miss any necessities or accessories to complete the statement. Lynn did the girls' hair one day before the funeral, but it needed to be touched up a little on the day of, as Nicole now thinks. Their Aunt Lynn was not a hairstylist by any means, and Lisa wasn't having it at all, so Lynn picked her hair out into an afro style, left alone basically. Florence regularly took her daughters to a lady named Candy, who did hair in her home on a street near Dexter Avenue, somewhere on Detroit's Northeast side. Nicole remembers her twin Michelle crying when she got her hair done, then all smiles afterward.

As put together as they were, it did not make them ready for that day. After the girls were dressed, Tommy rounded them up and out of the house. They left home, headed over to Florence's mother's home to meet with everyone riding in the family funeral cars. They got there before the hearse arrived. Entering the house was different this time. Nicole almost did not want to go in. Everyone inside was trying to be strong every time they looked at Nicole, Michelle, and Lisa. It was obvious that they all were hurting with them. Nicole felt that these people were trying to be strong for them, like she was for her sisters.

The house was filling up with more people by the minute. At one time, a cluster of people surrounding Florence's mom shared hugs and so much compassion. Nicole realized later that they were consoling her grandmother, as they learned of her decision not to attend her own daughter's funeral service. It was hard for everyone to witness this unfortunate heartbreak that a mother had to endure. Nicole tried not to cry much, and instead spent her time consoling her sisters, who were a major concern. Witnessing other friends and family members managing to keep a straight face during this horrific pain gave Nicole bursts of strength and courage between her moments of sorrow.

Before she could sit long enough to sink herself in sorrow, she heard someone yell, "They're here!" Her heart sank instantly. Tommy said, "Come on Nikki, Mimi, and Lisa. It's time to go." He gestured them over to their Grandmother Lurlee first, to give her some hugs and kisses. It was an emotional moment that lasted longer than was expected, which made them all tearful. Nicole understood her dear grandmother not seeing her daughter off for the final time on earth. Due to Lurlee losing two children in three years. Florence's brother Jesse Jr. the family as well. Nicole knew and understood that her grandmother could not handle attending the funeral. All the understanding in the world could not have made it any easier to leave her grandmother behind. They cried as they departed.

Everyone began to find the car they were going to be riding in. Nicole remembers her Aunt Lynn riding in the family funeral car with her, her dad, and her sisters. She says there were more people probably, but some moments of that day are a blur to Nicole now. They all were in their respective transit and off to the funeral.

People were lined up on the city streets, greeting the family with loud cheers of love and compassion. The vehicles drove at a slower pace than normal giving the fans a chance to show their condolences because the church could not hold all the people interested in attending. By the time all the cars reached the church, there was the longest line of people Nicole would not have ever imagined. There were people everywhere holding self-made signs of endearment. Nicole remembers being instructed to stay in the car as along with everyone else.

FLORENCE

June 30 1943   February 22 1976

In Loving Memory
Of the late

FLORENCE BALLARD CHAPMAN

FRIDAY, FEBRUARY 27, 1976
At 2:30 P.M.

To Be Held At
New Bethel Baptist Church
8450 LINWOOD AVENUE

Rev. C.L. FRANKLIN, Pastor

NOTE: This is a replica of the original obituary.

The Untouchables

The security team that Berry Gordy, Jr. hired was outside, taming the crowd as best they could. They were not prepared for the pandemonium at large. The security signaled to the cars that they were ready to escort everyone inside the church. Once they all exited the vehicles and began to walk the path to the door, all the fans went crazy. They were crying and screaming out how much they loved Florence.

Nicole was in awe of it all. She felt saddened that her mom wasn't there to see and feel all her fans' love. Given the circumstances, Florence could not be in attendance the way her daughter envisioned in her momentary daydream. This was her first time seeing her mother's fans in such a state, filled with love and empathy. It felt great to Nicole at that moment. She needed to feel that love. It gave her another boost, but at the same time, it only took a second to make her sad again, because the fans' reaction was because of the memorial for her mother.

Tommy grabbed his daughter Nicole's arm, saying, "Come on, Nikki," as she woke up from the daydream. No time for tears. She knew she had to keep moving. It was a painful realization, but she wore her game face.

The large security team escorted the Ballard/Chapman and Motown family in and outside of the church. Gordy paid for the cars, security, and maybe more. Nicole remembers for certain that "Poppa" Gordy specifically catered the limo service for Florence's final bout. "Poppa" Gordy was what Florence's daughters grew up calling Mr. Berry Gordy. The service was pretty lengthy in time, and sentimental. The father of Aretha Franklin—the Queen of Soul— Reverend Franklin, delivered the eulogy for Florence. Nicole remembers listening to his every word with her undivided attention. She was focused when anyone stood up to speak about her mother. She wanted to hear what people had to say about her mom. Reverend Franklin spoke the longest. His delivery gave Nicole more comfort and hope. She understood all that he said, and appreciated the message he delivered. She appreciated the compassion and concern he shared with her family. She was touched.

During the funeral service, the fans were rude to Diana, which Florence's family was not proud of and were not in agreement with. Diana was present and sincere. The burial process was a different round. It was direct and quick. Nicole has short memories of it, merely capturing the important moments involved. She remembers pulling up to a large cemetery with cars lined up and parked alongside the grass. They all got out of their vehicles to meet at Florence's burial plot. It was cold in Detroit on this day, so it was not the most pleasant visit for more reasons than one. Nicole thought to herself, "This is her final goodbye to her mom."

Everyone took their time stepping up to speak to Florence. Some were alone, while others coupled and grouped together. Diana Ross was alone as she tossed roses on Florence's casket, sharing her final moment with her dear friend here on earth. Once everyone had their moment, Tommy and his daughters stepped up one last time before they all gathered in prayer and headed back to their cars. Nicole was so confused about leaving her mother out there to be buried in the ground, all alone. She thought to herself that this must be why they call this a final resting place. It hurt to drive away, knowing she would never see her mother again. All the cars slowly drove right out of the cemetery. It was a dreadful feeling. It felt final for Nicole.

Forever Faithful

Everyone met up at a restaurant on Telegraph near Eight Mile. Nicole cannot think of the name of the restaurant. This is the time that ends the home going celebration, what would be called the "repast." It's traditionally held at a church in the basement, or a banquet hall area, but could be at a community center or even someone's home. Anywhere the mourners can gather to eat together and socialize, in honor of the decedent.

By then, it was expected that they all were ready to eat. Nicole remembers being so anxious and ready to get out of the car and go inside the restaurant, but no one moved when the car parked. There was a safety protocol enforced by their security team hired for that day. Every vehicle had to be parked before one door could be opened. Nicole does not recall who was standing outside of their car first as much as she does all of them entering the restaurant together as a unit.

They were treated special upon entry. They were compassionately servicing them all with much respect to the mourners of Florence Ballard Chapman, as they celebrated her life and legacy. Most, if not all of Motown, were in attendance, from head to the lower level of the operation, with the exception of Diana Ross. Nicole does not remember seeing Mary Wilson there, either, but she's not absolutely certain. A few people within their private party were employees of Motown who held various positions there. No one at Motown was excluded from the celebration of Florence. The energy there was happy and loving. It seemed as if the entire restaurant was booked for a private repast.

Nicole didn't notice regular business happening besides them, but she could have missed it while adjusting to her new reality. She was seated in the biggest section of the restaurant. Everyone was talking and laughing with one another before she ultimately ordered and ate. Several people made it over to the grieving girls and Tommy during the wait, offering their condolences. It was evident to Nicole that losing her mother was a shared loss. She found herself feeling sad for others for a moment before her own pain would resonate again. Nicole enjoyed everyone sharing their stories, keeping her mother's memory alive. It was comforting.

The food started coming from all angles. Nicole does not remember what she ate, but she recalled that it did not stop once the food started coming out until they were completely served. The talking never stopped. It was good seeing everyone having such a good time. That's what made Nicole's bitter moment sweet. Nicole was full and depleted. It must have been written all over her face, because her Aunt Lynn leaned over to her and asked if she was ready to go. Nicole nodded that indeed she was. Before long, Tommy asked for everyone's attention.

He expressed his gratitude for all of the love and support showed towards him, his daughters, adding Florence's mother, siblings, and family. This is Nicole's interpretation of her dad's thank you speech, since she cannot remember it verbatim.

They were finally leaving and in the car, riding home. This was when everyone said their goodbyes, or bye for now, and wished everyone safe travels heading back home. Some family and friends came from other states. Nicole remembers having knots in her stomach all the way home, thinking about her mom not being there when they open the door.

The celebration continued when they got home. Just when Nicole thought it was all over, everyone's started showing up to their house. Florence's sisters were inside setting things up around the house, to make the guests feel comfortable. They put food and desserts out that were donated, and dropped off to them for the guests. Before long, their house was filled with people and love. It just felt so weird to Nicole not having her mom there. Nicole relaxed on the sofa, where she sat back comfortably and watched everyone interacting, telling stories about her mom, laughing and having a good time. Some of the time, she felt too sad to laugh or smile, but she felt warm inside. Nicole saw more sad faces in that one day than she had seen in her lifetime. She just wanted everyone to be all right. Her dad was hurting, her grandmother was broken, her sisters kept crying, family and friends kept calling, and everyone kept talking and laughing so loudly it began to irritate her in some ways. She just wanted it all to stop!

All that love in the house, without her mom present, made her weak. Tears began to stream down her face. She felt like she couldn't mourn her mother for watching the world mourn her mom. It was an overwhelming feeling that captivated her emotions, and she was not sure if it was going to end. Stevie Wonder walked over to little Nicole with an empathetic notion of love. He hugged her and said, "Don't cry, I got y'all, everything will be ok." That meant so much to Nicole, because she knew if she ever needed to reach out to him, he would be there for them. She kept a special place for him in her heart because she knew it was sincere and genuine. Although she never did reach out to the man, she grew up calling "Uncle" Stevie. The comfort in knowing his sentiment was sufficient enough for her.

Nicole and her sisters were then ushered off to their room. It was getting late, and time for the girls to get some sleep. Florence's sisters cleaned up the kitchen and straightened up around the house before they left. The party was finally winding down and would be over soon. Some people stayed over longer than others, getting along beautifully as if there weren't ever any problems amongst any of them. Nicole and her sisters were already in bed by the time the last of their guests left. The house began to get quieter by the minute, which gave Nicole a more peaceful time to think. She thought about how kind all the people had been to them. She is ever so grateful for all the kind gestures demonstrated by their neighbors, friends, and family. It was necessary for the aid in all of their healing, and it meant a lot.

Happy thoughts make a person feel strong, and Nicole was glad to have them because she had more than enough sad thoughts embedded in her. Sad thoughts made her feel weak, lost, and distraught. Later on, in her life, Nicole found herself stuck in the sad thoughts for longer periods of time, which was not good for her.

Florence Ballard Chapman Through Nicole's Eyes

Nicole saw her mother as a relaxed person most times. She was fun and loving when she wasn't setting someone straight due to her low tolerance for bullshit. Florence liked to socialize and spend time with friends and family, but she never made a fuss over wardrobe or makeup. If she could have, Florence would have gone out on that stage and given it to her fans raw. No wig, makeup, or fancy gowns.

She was an in-the-moment type and always ready. If she felt it, she would give a show at any given moment, without needing the glitz and glamour. Nicole inherited that same characteristic behavior. She is the daughter that carried her mother's traits most, compared to her sisters. Nicole held onto every memory made with her mom, missing the bond they shared. Their bond grew through the turmoil and disruption that plagued their lives in such a short stretch of time. She witnessed her mother do nice things for people at random and heard some stories, but she felt her mother's acts of kindness are for the recipients to announce, as it was their moment, and they had the facts to share.

It's evident that Nicole didn't always witness how the quarrels between her parents would start, but she knows her mom would say what she felt without sugar-coating any of it. As a child, Nicole did not understand the pressure her mother dealt with. She was a child with a keen and mature mind that allowed her to put two and two together and sometimes predict the outcomes after her parents' unfortunate situations. Nicole paid attention to watching her parents closely, especially her mother. She saw what was going on at all times pretty much. Nothing got past Nicole. It was a known fact that Florence was a firecracker who would pop off easily if triggered. Tommy was usually the trigger that got her sparks going.

Nicole had overheard some of her family members mentioning her father, Tommy, to be a womanizer as well as a cheater to some extent. These accusations remained just that, as Nicole never found any truth to these rumors. If it was relevant, it never surfaced, and no outside children have ever been mentioned or recognized. She knows that her father disappointed her mom so often that her mother was beginning to give up on him.

Nicole can attest to the love her parents had for each other was real, but also a possessive love at times. Florence loved being loved, but was not a docile, mundane woman by any shape or form. Florence stood up to Tommy and may have thrown the first blow in some instances. Florence was explicitly verbal and not afraid to fight. Submitting to Tommy was out of the question.

CHAPTER DOS

TOMMY

Thomas "Tommy" Chapman, born January 28, 1940, and died May 11, 1985. It is unsure where Tommy originated from. Because there is little history known about Tommy, his daughter Nicole chose to share her father's life in detail, to give him character other than what has been described by others.

Tommy had a lonely and distant life growing up that was sure to distort some of his decision-making, determining outcomes in his life. He was abandoned as a baby when someone left him on a doorstep. Somehow, he ended up with a family that cared for him, gave him love, and raised him. Nicole remembers meeting her dad's friend, Spidey Turner, whose mom was like a mom to Tommy. There was also a lady in Spidey's family that Nicole remembers. She and her sisters called this lady Auntie Mickey. Nicole is not sure if Spidey or any of his family knew of her dad's passing. She looked for them at the funeral, but didn't see anyone. Tommy never found his birth mother or family. Who would know where to start to try to find any of Tommy's bloodline? As a grown man, Tommy was stern and private. He did not speak on his past much at all. Tommy was a husband and father. Tommy loved his family.

Not-So-Lucky Number Seven

So how does a seven-year-old live without her mother? Nicole was about to find out. The show was over, and they were back to their regularly scheduled program. Sometimes, Nicole would feel strong, which never lasted long enough to forget about the pain. She wanted so bad to feel better right then, to never feel sad again. "It was and is depressing as hell," Nicole remembered.

Things did change rather quickly. Life, as they knew it before, was no more. For Tommy, it was a deep hurt watching his daughters miss their mother. That's one thing Tommy would not have ever wanted for his three darling daughters. This prompted him to try a new way to carry on with his life by replacing their mom with babysitters, all of whom turned out to be total nightmares. The girls were not so lucky to get a loving and caring stepmom in their lifetime. It would have been too soon and hardly accepted at that time anyway. A mother figure of some sort was not desired from the daughters of Florence and Tommy.

One day after school, on the way home, Tommy told his daughters that he had someone there for them to meet. They were excited, and asked him who it was. Tommy explained that he would have a nanny at the house to be with the girls from now on. He said he needed help with them so he could get back to work, desperately seeking some normality. He said the nanny would cook and clean too, but the girls still needed to clean up behind themselves.

They understood and accepted their responsibilities. Nicole was anxious to see who was in their home, claiming these new duties for them. Not that Nicole was happy about it, she just went along with it. To be honest, she was not ready for this change. When they walked through the door, the nanny was front and center, waiting for them. Nicole does not remember feeling anything while first meeting her, but she will never forget how she made her feel soon after. Tommy introduced them, "Girls, this is Trudy, and she's going to look after y'all while I'm working." Depending on Tommy's schedule, Trudy would be required to stay late, or even overnight sometimes. She was a brown-skinned, round face, Afro-American, nice shaped lady around Tommy's age. She was what some call thick, to describe a desirable overweight body frame or structure. She wore her medium length hair in a ponytail every day.

Simple and plain was the name of her game. She was kind when meeting Florence's daughters, giving hugs and all. Quickly, she told them to wash their hands, then come eat. When they walked in the kitchen, Trudy made their plates and placed them on the table before them, just like Florence did when she fed her children. Tommy did not join them for dinner. He was in a hurry to get back to work. Nicole cannot remember what they ate that day for the life of her, because she could not stop thinking about this lady in her mother's kitchen trying to feed them. It just was not the proper visual for Nicole, and did not feel right to her. She managed to behave, and got through it without incident. When they finished eating, it was time to feed their pet fish, Momo, and Bobo.

They washed their hands, then met their father Tommy at the fish tank. He picked them up one at a time to place them over the tank slightly. The girls loved the view from the top, as it was like you were closer to the fish, looking directly into the water versus watching through the glass.

Feeding Momo and Bobo was Nicole and Michelle's light. The way the fish would race to the top of the water to eat those stinky pieces of dry flakes was amusing to the girls. Their time was cut short because Tommy had to leave. He gave his daughters a snack after feeding the fish, but the specifics are unknown, the act was ritualistic. It was a peanut butter and jelly sandwich most likely. Tommy loaded the girls with other goodies too. The girls pulled out their coloring books and crayons as their dad got them settled in upstairs. The girls were equipped with plenty of toys to play with and a television to watch in their bedroom if they wanted. There was no need for them to go downstairs anymore that night, besides going to the bathroom.

Tommy was getting ready to leave, so he stood at the bottom of the steps and called the girls down for hugs and kisses before leaving. He told them to behave and he would be back soon. They knew their daddy had to go back to work because that is what they were accustomed to. They just were not ready to separate so soon.

Nicole never witnessed her dad having any interest or intimacy with Trudy by the way, although she did seem quite relaxed as she moved about their home. Nicole wasn't so sure about Ms. Trudy, but she was willing to give her a chance. Nicole really did not have a choice. She does not remember how many days Trudy worked as their nanny, she just remembers the first and the last day with total accuracy.

Trudy's last day started with Tommy dropping the girls off at home where Trudy was waiting. He didn't walk his daughters in this day. He told them he was on the clock and had to leave immediately. "Behave" was always his last word to them, besides "I love you." Nicole and Michelle got out of the car and ran to the door. It was freezing out and Nicole remembers her face being so cold.

They walked into the house, hung their coats up and took off their boots. As soon as Nicole looked up from taking her boots off, she saw Trudy coming around the hallway holding baby Lisa. They spoke which could be described as dry. Lisa lunged for Nicole, so she grabbed her, and they went upstairs to their room.

A few minutes later, Trudy called on the girls to come downstairs to eat. Nicole was first to get down the steps, but Michelle and Lisa were only a few steps behind. Nicole was headed to the kitchen when she met up with Trudy in the hallway. It was a weird interaction and somewhat scary the way she just appeared before this fragile child, holding aluminum foil in the palm of her hand. Trudy got close to Nicole's face and opened the foil while saying, "Here is your dinner."

Trudy displayed Momo and Bobo's lifeless bodies on aluminum foil, as if they had been cooked. The fish looked dry and shriveled which made it obvious that they were dead and possibly burned. It was not clear what that insane woman did to those goldfish. Did

Trudy literally cook them? Nicole wasn't sure, but seeing Momo and Bobo dead made Nicole very angry. Trudy laughed directly in Nicole's face. Nicole yelled at her, "You're mean!"

With her sisters Michelle and Lisa quickly approaching, Nicole immediately screamed for them to go back upstairs! Michelle and Lisa did not see the fish as closely as Nicole did, but they knew something was wrong with the fish after hearing Nicole's tone of voice and seeing her face. Nicole still speaks about this angrily, stating that, "That bitch was jealous of our fish!" Trudy was jealous of the connection the girls had with their pet, and wildly envious of the attachment to their mother that came with those fish. Trudy was also jealous of the way Tommy catered to his daughters during their fish feeding and bonding time. Trudy had no respect or compassion for Tommy's young, scarred, motherless daughters.

What Nicole and her sisters endured was so traumatic that they ran upstairs and cried, but not too loud as for Trudy to hear them. They did not want any more interacting with her. Not one more word did they have for that evil vindictive lady. Nicole did confirm to her sisters that their goldfish were dead. As the girls cried, mourning yet another loss, Nicole could not help but call Trudy so many bad names that she made up a few. If she could have, she would have slapped Trudy's face clean off.

Shortly after, they heard someone coming up the stairs. They were shaking in the hopes that it was not the nanny from hell. That thought began to disappear as Nicole listened closely and noticed that it felt like her father Tommy by the way he walked up the stairs. He usually called out to the girls, but this time he was quiet, so they weren't sure if it was Trudy or their daddy. They watched the top of the step like a hawk.

When they saw it was their daddy, they all yelled and ran to him, grabbing him and crying. He said, "Hey, hey, what's the matter, what's wrong?" He picked Lisa up then they all blurted out, "Our fish daddy! They're dead! She killed them!" Tommy said, "What?! Who?!" The girls said, "Trudy did, daddy!" Tommy rushed down the steps in a way the girls had never witnessed before this day. They heard him speaking angrily to Trudy. This crazy lady had the nerve to fuss back at him. They were fussing while the girls were crying.

It felt like the girls could finally release all the anger they had built up in themselves towards Trudy. Nicole could not hear specifically what was said during her father and their hired nanny's argument, but Trudy was fired on the spot and never came back. They may have had a few days before nanny number two was hired. This time it was a man. This was not a man that any of the girls knew of prior to his sudden employment as their nanny. Nicole could not imagine how this man even became an option, besides her dad being desperate to replace the first nanny.

This nanny wasted no time with making Nicole feel uncomfortable. She tried not interacting with him, but he always seemed to need her to do something. Nicole couldn't make a move without this man touching her in some way. When he touched her arm, back or hand for instance, it felt weird. He quickly elevated to fondling her. He would touch her butt in passing and rub up against her with his private part. Needless to say, Nicole was eventually full-on molested by this man. He stuck around longer than any other nanny. Go figure. Nicole saw him look at her sister Michelle with a blank stare sometimes. She didn't know if he was thinking about touching her, or what. She just knew it was something that wasn't good, so she kept her sisters away from him.

Nicole endured a lot during this period, and kept her mouth closed about the molestation and constant fondling. She knew it was not right, but she did not have the courage to speak up. Nicole felt responsible for Michelle and Lisa and their safety. She was not going to let anything happen to her sisters for as long as she is alive. To this day, neither of Nicole's sisters have mentioned any unjust acts upon them by any of their caregivers. Michelle and Lisa have never heard about what you have just read, either.

One day, Tommy picked his daughters up from school and told them that their Aunt Lynn would be watching them today. Nicole asked him where the male nanny was without mentioning his name. Her dad said, "He's gone and not coming back." Nicole looked up to the sky and said, "Thank you God!" She closed her eyes and thought of her mom while tears rolled down her cheeks. She just wished her mom was still there with them. None of this would have ever happened had her mother Florence still been alive.

Nicole never told her dad what nanny number two did to her. She knows Tommy would have tried to kill that man. It was always unclear why he was no longer caring for the girls. Nicole was just glad that it was over, and he was gone. It is so hard for Nicole to even speak this man's name. She decided not to share his name for personal reasons, which we have respected.

There were a variety of babysitters thereafter. This string of sitters were mainly family members and friends who were considered family. This made things more like it was before Florence passed away. Nicole was better able to deal with the loss of her mom being under the care of family. Yet still, Nicole was so ready to leap right out of 1976.

I'm All Yours Until Tomorrow

Being a single parent for Tommy was more difficult than he thought it would be. It wasn't easy for him, but having support from Florence's family made it manageable for a while. Sometimes, it seemed to Nicole that her dad was overwhelmed. Things started to change in the way the Chapman's did things.

By the end of the summer, the girls were spending more time with their family and less time at home. Tommy had enough free time to go to work and do whatever else he wanted. The new life for Tommy was not easy. It became a constant struggle in different ways. The struggles he endured lasted throughout, and long after his daughters were out of his primary care. Money management was never a credential of Tommy's, which led him to lose pretty much everything that he and Florence had accomplished together.

Tommy felt a sense of depletion. There was nothing left in Detroit, Michigan for him, other than his three beautiful daughters. Nicole remembers a day when her dad took her and her sisters over to their grandmother Lurlee's house to stay, because he couldn't raise them on his own anymore. Tommy told his mother-in-law Lurlee that he would sign custody papers, giving her total control and rights to everything dealing with his and Florence's three daughters. He lost the house and didn't have much money left.

Tommy decided to leave Michigan in 1977 for a new start in Baton Rouge, Louisiana. Nicole was sad to see her dad go, but was pleased to stay with her grandmother instead. Nicole also felt her mother would have wanted her and her sisters to stay with their grandmother versus their father, anyway. Given the opportunity to honor her mother's wish, Nicole transitioned into the change effortlessly. Tommy made enough visits back to Michigan to make Nicole feel he never really left. Not that his visits were frequent, more that Nicole was satisfied with the frequency of them. Tommy sent money and bought his baby girls gifts often. There was a time when Nicole came home to gifts left on the porch for her and her sisters from their dad.

Florence's family had expressed lesser-than-equal value of Tommy because he did not meet their standards by doing as much as they felt he should have. Nicole understands their position and does not dispute it. She felt satisfied with the support of her father, and did not feel Tommy was neglectful. Nicole and her sisters spent many days and nights with their Aunt Maxine and her son, Chris. She remained a big part of their lives, continuing to be that loving aunt that she always had been before her sister Florence passed.

Florence and Maxine had been very close, and were together most of the time. Their birthdays were just eleven months apart. Aunt Maxine's son Chris and Florence's daughters grew up extremely close. These cousins are just as close as their mothers were. Chris also had a special relationship with his Aunt Florence, One he will never forget. He has many memories and funny stories to cherish for the rest of his life. They all went to church together on Sundays, just as they did when Florence was alive. The cousins saw one another even more after Florence's passing. Life simmered down somewhat for Nicole after her father left. She made it all the way through the rest of her elementary school days, before any more life altering episodes occurred.

The Rape of Nicole Chapman

By the time Nicole and Michelle reached middle school, their different personalities stood out. They were like night and day, but they understood each other well. School became an escape and pastime for Nicole. It kept her occupied and focused on her studies. Her mind didn't get a chance to wander much during school time.

Nicole was sociable, but didn't keep many friends. She and Michelle were teased and bullied by some of the meanest kids at their school. She never could understand why those kids wanted to bring harm to them, as if they weren't enduring enough life altering pain all on their own. Just when Nicole thought she was on a rhythm that worked for her sanity, here came another predator, identified as a student at her school.

This was a schoolmate that she recognized by face, but had no casual or intimate contact with. When she saw him come around the stairway, she thought nothing of it. Before she could think about what was happening, he snatched her. He twisted her wrists so painfully it caused her to scream so loud that she was sure someone had to have heard her. He kept trying to cover her mouth with his hand but Nicole bit, scratched and punched him repeatedly as he took her into the school corridors. He told Nicole to shut up and, for some nerve-wrecking reason, she did. She knew once she was inside that corridor that no-one was going to hear her or even see them, because this particular corridor was seldomly used.

Nicole tried resisting him and his demands for her to remove her clothes, but he was aggressive and overpowering. He dominated her mind and body with force and an evil look in his eyes. Nicole became still as she sunk into a trance. He told her not to scream or he would hurt her. That's when she checked out mentally and just let it happen, so it could hurry and end. To be raped was embarrassing, and she couldn't understand why that kept happening to her. She actually thought he was playing and kidding around when he approached her. She wishes she had taken him seriously the moment he invaded her space, and fought him harder from the start. It happened so fast that it could not have been more than ten minutes total. His actions totally threw Nicole off guard. She never imagined she could or would get raped at school. When he finished, he jumped up quickly, pulled up his pants and ran out of the school doors exiting the building.

Nicole got up and ran the opposite way inside the school doors, redressing herself in such a desperate, embarrassing manner. She ran until she made it to the school's office. She entered the office frantic, shaking and in tears. One of the ladies in the office spoke to Nicole, asking if she was alright. Nicole tried responding, but all the while, the school's secretary saw Nicole's face from the moment she came in the office. She noticed Nicole was distraught and disheveled, so much so it concerned her. She abandoned her work to assess Nicole's behavior.

When she approached Nicole, she asked, "What happened to you?" Nicole started talking and did not stop. She answered all of the questions asked. Once the school secretary heard Nicole out, she took her directly into the counselor's office to handle the issue properly. The secretary informed the counselor of the severity that was in front of her without giving details. That is when Nicole gave her statement, and the first initial report was made. The counselor called the police and Nicole's grandmother, who was Nicole's legal guardian at that time. The school secretary notified the school guards who went to search for the alleged assailant right away, but did not find him. Mrs. Lurlee Ballard and her daughter Lynn made it to the school before the police. They were not aware of the actual incident.

The school counselor notified Mrs. Lurlee that her granddaughter had an experience that day that required her immediate attention. Nicole's grandmother was afraid of what she would hear concerning her granddaughter. The school secretary escorted Nicole's family into the counselor's office, where Nicole remained in privacy. Seeing Nicole's face, and how troubled and shaken she was, brought her grandmother to tears. She went from a concerned grandmother to an angry one, once she learned of what happened to her granddaughter. Grandma Lurlee decided that they were not going to sit there and wait for the police. It was imperative that she get her granddaughter to the hospital for a proper examination, testing and collecting viable evidence behind this random act.

As they were leaving, they bumped into the police entering the school. The officers insisted that they stay and give an official report. They all complied and went back into the office. After the official police report was taken, Nicole and her family were free to go to the hospital, which they did with no hesitation. Nicole's family didn't waste any time getting justice for Nicole either. They supported her all the way throughout the criminal case proceedings. Her family never doubted her or left her side. Even though Nicole's sisters did not know about the nanny molesting her, they knew about her being raped at her middle school. Nicole thinks her sister Michelle would have been quicker than she was in a situation like that. She wished her sister could have been there to protect her that time.

Nicole thought the boy may have been playing with her for the first second or so, when she should have never allowed her space to be invaded by him, even if jokingly so. The rapist was apprehended soon after the incident and ultimately sentenced. Justice was served, and Nicole put that life-altering moment behind her, vowing to never let that interfere with her future. She never bumped into that boy again. This is when Nicole's grandmother informed her of what happened to her mom Florence when she was young herself. Nicole did not know her mom had been raped before. Lurlee gave her granddaughter a box with newspaper articles inside, which included the story about her mom being sexually assaulted. She wanted to know everything she could find out about the man who'd violated and tormented her mother. Over time, thorough research provided this information shared with you.

The Rape of Florence Ballard

Reggie Harding was the named rapist, as stated in many different sources, including Wikipedia. The crime took place in the Springtime on a warm Monday night in 1960, when Florence and her brother Billy went to The Graystone Ballroom Jazz club together. After being there for some time, Florence and her brother parted ways, socializing with other guest mates.

Many familiar faces were in the crowd, making the place rather comfortable for Florence. She enjoyed her time there, until she was ready to leave. Florence looked for her brother, but in the midst of of three thousand people, her unsuccessful search grew tiresome. Florence decided to go ahead, leave without her brother and just walk home alone. Florence lived about eleven blocks away, in The Brewster Douglas Projects. The walk home would have been an approximate twenty-four-minute walk to her home. It is assumed that Reggie noticed Florence as a member of the "Primettes," and offered her a ride home.

Reggie was also popular for his success on the Eastern High School's basketball team. Florence knew who Reggie was and accepted his offer without real concern. It's not known if Florence was aware of the accusations of him being a serial rapist, or his recent charge for statutory rape on a 15-year-old girl when he was 18. Reggie was tried but acquitted after his defense argued that the intimate act was consensual. Reggie was considered a tall, handsome, stunning young man who had no trouble getting female companions. He was admired by women of all types, young and older, all desiring his attention. It's too bad that some ladies had to experience the ugly side of him that many people in the area had heard rumors about, although they seemed unsure about it for a while.

Unfortunately, Florence found out for certain when Reggie drove off with her and went the wrong way down Woodward Avenue. He acted as if he was going to turn around, but instead, he took an ill-fated turn around the block and parked in a vacant lot, where he raped Florence at knife point.

A small petite 16-year-old Florence faced off with the seven-foot-tall and two hundred pounds of terror aggressing her. He didn't waste any time letting Florence get out of the car when he was finished. He didn't waste any time getting out of sight as well. Florence got out of his car and ran home as fast as she could. She was upset and ashamed, crying all the way home and feeling guilty for accepting a ride from Reggie. As soon as she walked through the door, she shut the world out and dealt with her situation internally. Who knows what Florence thought and felt in that moment?

She shared what happened to her with her family and kept quiet about it for months before even telling her group mates. She didn't share much about this situation ever. It was actually cut and dry, with no real play involved. It happened so fast and it was unbelievable to her that it happened the way that it did. It's unknown exactly when Florence told her family, or who she talked to first about it but once she spoke up, she told the necessary people she felt should know. Florence and her family wanted to prosecute Reggie, but no one is sure why she did not get her due justice for his vicious act on her. That one terrifying moment affected the rest of her life.

Who Was Reggie Harding?

Reggie was born to a young teenage mom who was forced to give him up for adoption at birth. A Caucasian couple adopted him. Raising him was challenging. Understanding that he was a troubled child brought about compassion from his adopted parents. Reggie committed petty larceny type crimes as a youth. His adopted parents thought they had better make some changes because their son was out of control. In 1959, his parents sent him to a cherry-picking farm in Cadillac, Michigan in hopes of breaking the pattern he had so diligently practiced. Instead, he stole the farmers truck and made his way back to the life he knew best in Detroit.

    Reggie stayed a short time there with others that did not fully accept his presence. It was uncomfortable for Reggie. He worked from his own rules and showed no concern for how his decisions made others feel. This act of destructive behavior was a pattern of Reggie's. How far he would go seemed to be much farther each time. Reggie's parents could not have been proud of his current and constant divide, but they did not give up on him when he returned home from the Cherry Farm up north. What, if any, punishment was imposed for his dishonorable acts is unknown. He returned to school at Eastern High School in Detroit and put his height and basketball skills to use.

    The rest of that year went great, as he became a local sensation bringing Eastern High to a Basketball Championship. Reggie went on to win two more Basketball Championships with his school in 1960 and 1961. Reggie was a trophy for the City of Detroit.

    By the time Reggie reached his senior year in high school, he was honored in the newspapers as one of the best basketball players in the country. After Reggie graduated in 1961, he went to a prep school in Tennessee for some time, then a few semi-pro basketball leagues before he was drafted into the National Basketball Association (NBA). He was the first basketball player drafted without ever playing for any college teams. He officially played for his home team, the Detroit Pistons from 1963 -1967, where he was highlighted for averages of 11+ and 12+ points each game. In 1963 and 1964, Reggie continued his neighborhood socializing in between games, with no regard for the preparation of his schedule. He continued his same rambunctious behavior, giving him legal issues. The legalities caused Mr. Reggie Harding an entire season. He was suspended for the 1965 - 1966 season.

The next season was not so good for status quo on the Pistons. This downward spiral began when Reggie was traded to the Chicago Bulls in 1967 for a total of fourteen games, winning two, losing twelve. He was then traded again, but this time to the Indiana Pacers of the American Basketball Association (ABA) League in 1968. He was traded and signed in 1967, but did not play his first game as an Indiana Pacer until January 20, 1968.

Reggie's game by now was literally off-point. His stats dropped continually, which caused him to be passed around from team to team. Reggie's constant criminal antics and misconduct on the teams garnered him fines and repercurssions for missing practices and such. Reggie was not the obedient one when it came to following the rules in the game, nor in life. He played the game, but wasn't a game player. He was paid $300 per game for his final few years in his NBA career after agreeing to a reduced contract, declining salary pay. All the fines and restrictions caused more loss of income, leaving him in the red when his basketball career finalized. Reggie actually owed the NBA money.

Reggie had some success in life, but lived a rambunctious lifestyle with insurmountable uncanny incidents shaping his character into a self-destructive one. Reggie was quite the character. He was insecure, arrogant, rude, disrespectful and violent with a sense of entitlement, expecting favor everywhere he went because of the fame he was awarded from his basketball hype. Reggie loved the streets just as much as basketball. He never let one go without the other. Along with the street interaction coupled with drugs and crime, Reggie stayed in night clubs so much that he would be there before and after games and practices, sometimes skipping practices due to this routine of his. He was a drinker, used drugs, women and committed more crimes than we will ever know. Some assumed crimes have always been rumored, but never truly validated. Validation was not needed to shape thoughts of this young man, as some of the rumors affected his turnout in the end.

Reggie was known to carry a gun with him in his gym bag wherever he went, including basketball practices and games, but no one was brave enough to confront him to check his bag. There were not enough assistant coaches or affiliates back then to keep an eye on Reggie, or any players troubled this much. Reggie's gun cases and assault charges were piling up rapidly. His radical ways made his teammates feel uncomfortable and unsafe around him, because he was too unpredictable and careless.

There was an incident with fellow basketball mate Jimmy Rayle, where Reggie threatened him and pulled his gun because he felt Mr. Rayle was racist, saying, "Aye Tweetie Bird, I hear you hate niggers." This outright ludicrous act angered other players on Reggie's team, making them want to distance themselves from him. If that wasn't enough to end his professional basketball career, threatening to kill the Pacers General Manager Mike Storen, during a live television interview, did. Reggie was out of everyone's control besides the law.

Reggie went on with his career-less life, penniless and back on the rough unkind streets of Detroit, Michigan, where he explored with drugs heavier than before. It's been said that he was using heroin, amongst other drugs. Reggie continued a life of petty crimes and ended up doing two years in the Jackson State Prison for parole violation. Another infamous incident is the repeated robbery of a local corner store that Reggie frequented. Reggie wore a skin tone stocking over his face and demanded money from the store attendant at gun point. After complying with the robber's demands, he asked, "Reggie, is that you?" The seven-foot Reggie replied, "Naw man, it ain't me," while running out of the store.

Reggie started his last day alive hanging out with his friends on the corner, drinking and carrying on with nonsense when a guy he knew named Carl Scott wasn't liking some things Reggie said, which started an argument between the two. Reggie still thought he was the beloved trophy of all, but that had changed drastically by this time. Carl was no punk, and showed Reggie by slapping him in the face hard, but Reggie was a bully and embarrassed Carl by slapping him back, then picked up the much smaller Carl, extending him in the air, holding him up, taunting him in front of everyone there on the corner. Reggie was known to do this to people from time-to-time instead of fighting. It usually worked, but this time the laughter from others wasn't pleasing to Carl, sending him off in a rage.

Reggie was still standing on the corner of Kercheval Street and Parkview Street, talking to some girls. Carl returned with a gun in his hand, ready for revenge. He pointed the gun at Reggie. "If you gone shoot me, shoot me in the head, so I don't feel any pain," yelled Reggie. Carl shot Reggie, dropping the giant to the ground, where Carl then granted Reggie's wish with one shot to his head. This took place on a warm Wednesday evening on August 31, 1971. Reggie Harding died the next day on September 1, at Detroit General Hospital. His funeral was held at Greater Mount Carmel Baptist Church on Mack Avenue.

After reading all of the stories on Reggie Harding's life, Nicole remembered most of it verbatim. She cannot forget it, but what stuck with her most was how he was buried after he died. The burial plot was not dug out properly, shortening the measurements, causing his casket to be rested with a slant. His coffin was tilted with his legs elevated to some noticeable degree, and they left it that way. Nicole recognized that this had to be a horrible moment for his family, but she couldn't help but laugh a little when she read it. She had never heard anything like that ever. Made her feel like a bit of karma visited him in the very end. A dishonorable moment for him on his sendoff day to face The Creator gave her some satisfaction, if any could be given.

The Graystone

The Graystone Ballroom was a Jazz Club where the upper class gathered to dance and listen to live music located at 4237 Woodward Avenue. This historic musical landmark sat one block long, landing on the corner of Willis Street and Canfield Street in Detroit, Michigan.

SUPREME EXIT

The Graystone Ballroom opened on February 27, 1922. It had been long-awaited and highly anticipated after a few failed attempts over a number of years. There were plans to open up the Graystone with different business ventures inside, including a Chinese restaurant that was to be named "Chinese Gardens." Detroit's bandleader Jean Goldkette opted to design a corner of these five stories, one block long building, tackling the attached part of the building in the back, making it the infamous Graystone Ballroom with a sixty-foot beautifully decorated domed ceiling in the ballroom. You could watch the people dance and socialize from a balcony that ringed the ballroom dance floor below.

In the warm months, the guests enjoyed an evening of dancing in the extended garden area of the Graystone Gardens. This sock hop spot collected upwards of 3,000-plus patrons each night they were opened. The staircase was marbleized, with hand-carved stair railings leading to a beautifully crafted circular fountain. There were many convenient and comfortable areas at every turn inside the Graystone Ballroom, making guests sure to feel luxurious. There were six storefronts along with an elegant walkway long enough to feel like a hallway with cream-colored marble and stone pavement that led to the Graystone's office space, all of which faced Woodward Avenue.

The Graystone Ballroom was equipped with an in-house band, The McKinney's Cotton Pickers and Jean Goldkette's Orchestra in which they became nationally known but invited special guests often. People came out from all over, including from different cities and states, to catch some of the greatest performers booked at The Graystone Ballroom, such as Duke Ellington, Ella Fitzgerald, Billie Holiday, Count Basie, Guy Lombardo, and Glenn Miller, just to name a few. This was the Blues and Jazz era, with the soulful sounds of Motown creeping in. Ballrooms were known to be segregated, and so was the Graystone. Monday nights were the only time dedicated to Blacks.

After a few losses and different ownerships, none other than Mr. Berry Gordy Jr., equipped with the cash, credit, and Motown sounds, purchased The Graystone Ballroom in 1963 for $123,000. This would have been just three years after Florence Ballard was raped by Reggie Harding, leaving The Graystone Ballroom. Gordy purchased The Graystone building, where all of Motown entertainers were only allowed inside on Monday nights to party. Gordy himself was once a faithful patron who looked forward to Monday nights at Graystone. There were plenty of networking opportunities abroad. He saw the lights and owned the night. Gordy revived the spot and gave it all he had to offer until Motown music took him in a different direction. In 1972, Gordy moved Hitsville from its birth home of Detroit, Michigan, to Los Angeles, California. The management of The Graystone minimized over time as well as its priority. The fate was sealed when the demolition crew arrived on June 18, 1980, to erase the memories of so many near and far.

I Will Survive

Life for Nicole did continue after the rape, but it wasn't really living. Everything just happened in her life. Being past this point of no return forced her into coasting through life, living in a trance lead by robotic motions left on autopilot. She was there, but not present. Her mind stayed on things unsettling, intercepting her joy. That's when depression crept in, and when she needed counseling. She just wasn't herself anymore and felt different. Over time, the "old her" was but a memory. A fairytale, even. Her life seemed so perfect until everyone started leaving. A life becoming full of sadness and continually grieving made Nicole feel the need to get away.

Florence's mom Lurlee was a breast cancer survivor. After having a mastectomy, she remained in remission for ten years before cancer cells set up in her body again, but this time much more aggressively. Lurlee made it with her granddaughters through middle school, but barely made it to the top of high school before cancer returned to claim her. The deterioration was rapid.

Nicole was present and available for her grandmother. She did all that was required to help her grandma maintain as much comfort as possible. She was a big help to her aunts in caring for their mom. Lurlee was a fighter who stayed strong until the end. Nicole got a sick feeling on her grandmother's last day of life on earth. She felt the feeling was a sign to prepare her. She knew that her grandmother was slipping away from her. Nicole felt like she was losing another mother. Florence's mother took her last breath on October 8, 1982, at the age of 72. Her funeral service was held on Nicole and Michelle's fourteenth birthday, October 13, 1982.

Tommy came from Baton Rouge, Louisiana, to attend the home going service for his mother-in-law. He loved her and always respected her as his mother. He was concerned about his three daughters and their care beyond this point. Their Aunt Pat, Maxine, and Lynn assured Tommy that they would continue to care for his and Florence's daughters, that he would not have to worry about anything at all. The girls wanted to stay in Michigan with their aunts, but spent some time in Louisiana with their dad as well.

Going to Louisiana to visit their dad always gave Nicole weird feelings within. It was nice to get away, but it was just different. Tommy was always there waiting at the airport for his daughters, just as he was when they were in school. This time they met his new lady friend. He introduced her to them as Flo. Yes, her name was Flo, as well. Nicole never saw government credentials to confirm this to be her legal name, but it was what she answered to. She was genuinely kind to his daughters. She was kind to their father as well. She made them feel welcomed and comfortable. They had a lovely home, and things were cordial and quiet. It was weird seeing her father have intimate dealings with a woman other than her mother.

Nicole also noticed the two adults getting along and enjoying one another in a loving way. Sometimes, Nicole imagined staying with her dad and how it would be, now that he had a companion. Seeing how another lady would love him, and see how he treated her, was a wonder in Nicole's mind. She only knew how he was with her mother. To see her dad with a different woman that he appeared to care for was interesting to her. Would he be the same man he was with her mom, or had he changed into a better man was important for her to know?

She was a nice pretty lady who Nicole saw nothing but happiness from. "Flo probably would have been a nice stepmother to have gotten closer to," thought Nicole. There were moments when she would think about some of her dad's secrets, which always made her spirit take a turn for the worst. Nicole remembers some unspeakable, inappropriate things that created a different side to her dad. Tommy loved his wife and daughters, but could not have loved himself, considering some of his actions. Tommy was a lost soul in search of himself. His true self was necessary for him to know, but the possibility looked fruitless. Were his actions the result of what he went through as a child growing up? Was he dysfunctional from birth, or was he just a twisted individual by choice, selfishly feeding his ego, giving in to the evils of the world? Nicole prayed for God to have mercy on his soul.

A Boost

High school was a drag for Nicole. She didn't fit in is how she felt. She would skip school with her friends and drink beer with them. Drinking beer made her feel numb, which became her drink of choice, just like her mom, Florence. Nicole's aunts didn't know she was skipping school. She got away with it for a long while here and there before her Aunt Lynn found out and confronted her about it. Nicole couldn't lie to her aunt. She promised she would do better.

They started by moving Nicole from Henry Ford High School to Redford High School, and then Cooley High School. Nicole ran from her reality, while she ended up facing it again with every move. All of that bouncing around from school to school accomplished nothing. None of that was addressing the issue. By then, Nicole was lost and sunken in depression . It was around this time that their

Aunt Mary Wilson sent them a $1,500 check each. They had no idea it was coming. The girls thanked her, then began to think of what to spend it on. Nicole thought to herself how she could finally build a complete wardrobe that fit her style. She could now buy some things that she couldn't purchase before.

Nicole was into relaxed attire, like jogging suits and gym shoes for basic everyday wear. She had to have the latest Air Jordan shoes and have her hair done professionally. Nicole thinks she adapted the comfort in dressing so relaxed as not to attract attention from the boys. She was shy and was not thinking about dating, because of her experiences being violated. She also didn't think any boys would be interested in her because of how she dressed. The girls were so excited and happy that they couldn't wait to cash their checks and go shopping. Nicole was able to shop for what she wanted to dress herself the way she liked, which made her feel enthusiastic about going to school. Nicole gained a little more confidence with those few dollars. It helped build up her self-esteem also at that time. The money only lasted a few weeks before it was gone. The clothes, confidence, and self-esteem lasted a lot longer. Nicole was forever thankful and grateful to her Aunt Mary for that boost in her life. It was well needed.

Another Big Loss

Life had become consistently decent with many highlights, but tragedy didn't take long to return. Nicole was dealt one hell of a hand laced with heartache, beginning at age seven. She doesn't question her life, but she often wonders what could've been. On a beautiful Saturday evening, her Aunt Lynn came to her with unsettling news. She asked Nicole and her sisters to sit down so she could discuss something with them.

They had no idea what she was going to say, but it looked serious. She continued, repeating, "Your dad, your dad...," when Nicole interrupted and immediately asked, "Is he ok?" Lynn answered, "No, he passed." Nicole screamed, "NO! This can't be true!"

The girls were a mess. It was the day before Mother's Day (May 11, 1985) when Tommy passed. To get that news one day before one of Nicole's hardest days every year made the cycle of loss and hurt repeat. Mother's Day was a total wreck for the girls. Nicole wondered if her dad was with her mom in heaven. She wondered if her mom was with her mom Lurlee on that Mother's Day. There's probably no specific day when mothers are appreciated in heaven. In the King James's version of the Bible, 1 Corinthians 10:13 says, we will become supplied with the strength to endure and survive any burden we may feel is too heavy. That's the version minus the "ye," "thou," "hath" and a few other pronouns that bare the same meaning. Most people say it like this, "God won't put on you more than you can bear."

Well, Nicole wished God didn't trust her so much, testing her strength. That was a lot to bear, and too much when you totaled up her pain from tragic deaths in her short lifetime. She made it through all of it and more, which is a testament to the 1 Corinthians scripture mentioned. Nicole talked to God a lot growing up. They built a strong relationship early on in her life before her mom passed. She asked him to protect them and their hearts. She prayed to have a good night's sleep since she couldn't sleep anymore after losing her mom. She missed her mom and grandmother immensely.

Hearing the news of her dad's sudden passing was piercing to Nicole's soul. Her life was filled with tragedy after tragedy, with just enough time in between to coddle her into thinking things were good. She couldn't believe her daddy was gone. Once Tommy's lady Flo finished with his final arrangements, the Ballard family was notified immediately. Nicole felt so conflicted, thinking of things her dad did when she was younger, the things he did to their mom, and how some crazy way, it was still a fight not to love him.

Nicole's Uncle Willie (Billy) Ballard and his wife, Annie, flew with them to New Orleans for their dad's funeral service. Willie Ballard was Florence Ballard's older brother. It was the emptiest

Nicole had ever felt. Her dad was all she had left of an actual parent. When she saw her dad in that casket, she could have dropped right where she stood, but she needed to see him up close and examine him. Nicole was upset about hearing how her father supposedly died. She walked up to the casket in tears. She talked to her dad and examined him looking all around his face, neck, and head areas.

    At first sight, she did not see anything telling. She wanted to see him move so this could turn out to be a joke or something, but instead, she happened to glance at a sight she missed. This was when she saw the wound to his head where he'd been shot, which confirmed to her what they were told was true. Nicole could see the patching up they did to plug the hole on the left side of his head, near the temple area. All she could think at that point was, her dad is really dead! She felt weak at the knees at that moment. Nicole's Aunt Annie held her and started walking her away from the casket. She walked away thinking, "Who did this to my dad?!" She was angry. Her dad was murdered, and the truth had not come out.

    The Ballard family received a call notifying them that Tommy had been shot at a pool hall. They believed it. It was known to pretty much everyone, including his daughters, that Tommy hung out and socialized at pool halls. Who did it, and why is it still a mystery? Nicole overheard people making accusations that her fathers died from a heart attack. Tommy did not have a heart attack, stroke, or any other naturally fatal issues. Her dad died from one gunshot to his head.

    She never knew what caliber or type of gun was used, because this situation was sealed and covered up. She would love to know who was behind all of that, but she didn't push for information after a few people whispered to the Ballard family that it would be unsafe to probe. Nicole felt like most people didn't care much about her dad. Not enough to stand for his justice. She knew it would take her or her sisters to investigate their father's murder one day when they were old enough.

TOMMY

Nicole suddenly remembered Spidey, who was an adopted family member of her dad's. She is unsure if Spidey or any of Spidey's family members ever knew that her dad had died. Nicole also wondered if any of the Motown family was there. She looked around for all of them at the funeral, but she didn't see anyone she knew besides her dad's lady friend Flo, who was very sad and tearful. Nicole saw Flo being consoled by some people there that she knew. There were no other family members of Tommy's that any Ballard family had ever been aware of. Tommy never found his birth mother or family.

Who would know where to start to try to find any of Tommy's bloodline? That was all they knew about his life growing up. They said their goodbyes to the nice lady Flo, wished her well, then parted ways. The flight back home was heartbreaking for Nicole. She walked away, feeling like her back was turned to her father. She thought about how, at one time in her life, she wanted to grow up and kill her dad for hurting her mother. Now it felt like it was killing her that someone killed her dad. She felt helpless like she had never known before or since.

That was her most emotional trip ever. The further she got away from New Orleans, she felt like she was leaving her father back there alone. She felt so lost and empty, realizing again that she didn't have a living parent or grandparent anymore. Nicole's reality was a painful revelation. Everyone at home expressed their condolences to Nicole and her sisters. They remained supportive and compassionate throughout the girl's time of sorrow.

CHAPTER TRES

NICOLE

Nicole Chapman, born October 13, 1968, to Florence Glenda (Ballard) Chapman (June 30, 1943 - February 22, 1976) and Thomas "Tommy" Chapman (January 28, 1945 - May 11, 1985). Nicole is one of Florence and Tommy's oldest fraternal twin daughters. Michelle is her twin. Michelle is what people call a "diva." Some felt that the descriptive word "glam" should be Michelle's legal title before her first name like "Dr." Michelle, for instance. Nicole has a baby sister named Lisa Chapman, as well.

Lisa was four years old when Florence passed. Michelle and Nicole were seven. They were all teens by the time their dad Tommy died. Nicole did not see everything and did not know everything, so she only spoke about what she knows specifically. She has confirmed, corrected, and addressed as many of the rumors as she could. The memories that she has are true and evident, but personal and sensitive at the same time. Her prayer is that more readers than less appreciate her transparency. Nicole has been described as a kind, good hearted person who gives her all and her last to see others have. Nicole is emotional at times which can be expressed negatively. With the good and bad, we will sum it all up and say she is not where she wants to be today, but as long as she has tomorrow, she has another chance. She will not stop trying to do better, and to be better. She continues to pray that the spirits and energy surrounding her be a vessel to her healing process.

My Way

Adulthood was creeping up on Nicole. Soon she would be eighteen, making her responsible for her own actions. No parents to depend on or go to for advice. The Ballard family was as supportive as possible throughout the girls growing up. How things might change was a haunting thought for Nicole that faded shortly after.

As time progressed, she saw how her family never changed. Neither did the support amongst them all, but the responsibilities did change gradually. Besides working and cooking, Nicole didn't crave for much else. She had always been a homebody, often to a fault. It was way too easy to isolate herself, as it still is today. She never had to look for any company, because her family was always present. Nicole's mission was to find the peace she was in search of. The kind that she has yet to find.

Nicole stopped attending school slowly but surely, to the tune of one whole year's worth of random-to-consistent absences. Letters came and went. Nicole got them all before anyone could see them. Nicole's school counselor decided to do a welfare check on a student severely delinquent in attendance. The school's counselor called Nicole's home, and Lynn caught that call. She was informed of Nicole's educational status and the school's concern about her not being present. Lynn already had a clue about her niece skipping school here and there, but she was surprised to find out how serious the issue really was.

Lynn was close to her nieces, more like a big sister. She also had a lot of love for them after losing their mother so young. She often wondered if she had been too easy on them. Regardless, she had to immediately discuss this with her niece, because Lynn needed to understand what her niece was going through. They had tried a few different tactics with the other aunts, to no avail. Things were being misunderstood between the family members. Nicole became distant and withdrawn as she got older. With all this in mind, Lynn approached her niece with compassion and open-mindedness. Lynn never let an opportunity slip past without sharing some encouragement to do the right thing. It ultimately became Nicole's decision at will.

Nicole was a few months away from turning eighteen, so Lynn figured not to push too hard, being that she wasn't certain about the level of depression and mental confusion her niece was burdened with. Yes, Nicole agreed that finishing school would be the right thing to do, but she needed help with her mental status, to control of her fears and manage her sorrows.

All such depressive mannerisms were in her all through her high school days, and grew deeper each year. She tried running from them by transferring from one school to another as if it would alter her mental psyche in some favorable way and heal Nicole instantly. However, it didn't work out that way. For Nicole, at that time in her life, school gave off dreadful energy just being there, reminiscent of horrible moments in her life. Even the beautiful memories of her father always there to pick her up from school turned into horror as it would lead to the fact that it all ended in death.

Reality, to put it plain and simple. How to deal with this depression and suppression was what Nicole needed to know. She later found that she could tell herself something and believe it. She talked herself into awareness, facing her own adversities head-on. She was growing and learning firsthand. She learned from the mistakes made, just like most of us do. Her own, as well as other's mistakes, were enough examples for her to be forewarned.

Finding Love

There was no other feeling of excitement that Nicole could get when Motown called her to say that her mother Florence would be inducted posthumously into the Rock and Roll Hall of Fame on April 18, 1988. It was a definite honor to witness as Nicole and her family celebrated Florence's accomplishment. Nicole often felt like something was missing in her life. Nicole knew that she would one day soon find love, too. Love would probably have needed to be close to home, because Nicole did not go out much. She preferred being home but enjoyed venturing off to her friends' homes in the neighborhood sometimes, or she would walk up and down the street with her friends talking and being cute.

You couldn't tell Nicole she wasn't cute. She was attracted to her neighbor a few doors down from her house. She thought he was so fine, and she liked his style. Everybody knew she liked him by the way she acted when he was around. She denied it for as long as she could. She had no idea he was watching her, too. She quickly caught his awareness, and felt the vibe. They flirted and started hanging out together more often, then eventually began dating. They were a cute couple in love.

He was Nicole's first love. Their families were close, since everyone knew one another pretty much just from being neighbors for so many years. They got along well and had good times together. He was empathetic and gentle with Nicole, compassionate about the losses in her life. He was every bit of uplifting to Nicole. She was a beautiful, insecure, fragile, naive girl. He knew it and protected her in that sense. He wanted her to be happy and well. She was blessed to have a guy that wanted to love her in spite of the baggage she brought along into the relationship. Before long, Nicole and her boyfriend were pregnant and blessed with a healthy baby boy that they named De'Juan in June of 1988.

Nicole's Aunt Lynn knew Nicole was expecting before she did. Before Nicole could tell her Aunt Lynn, she blurted out to Nicole, "You're pregnant." She just looked at Nicole and said, "You are pregnant, I can tell." She told Nicole to go and buy a pregnancy test, and she did that day. Her Aunt Lynn was right. Nicole was pregnant. Again, Lynn decided to allow Nicole to direct her life by asking her what she would decide for her future. She assured Nicole that she would be supportive of any decision as long as it was her own.

Nicole's other aunts were just as supportive as well. They understood that Nicole was grown, and could make her own decisions. Needless to say, she wanted to become a dependable, loving, and nurturing mom. Nicole had no clue how to do it, but she watched her family care for children and helped with a few while growing up, so she knew she would figure it out just like everyone else does.

Nicole's son's father and his family were the kindest people she had ever met. She loved them, and they loved her and her son, De'Juan. A great family that welcomed her into their home and hearts until, one day, her son's father caught her and his best friend in a compromising position. Nicole was so embarrassed and ashamed. She took full responsibility for making senseless decisions. It was one of the biggest mistakes she had ever made in her entire life. Her son's father didn't deserve that, and his friend didn't deserve a piece of Nicole.

Nevertheless, this incident broke the first-time parent's lovely bond up indefinitely. Nicole's son's father tried to work things out with Nicole, but he could not commit. It was hard for Nicole at first. She didn't like to see him leave after visiting with their son. She missed spending quality time with her friend and former lover. She couldn't apologize enough for hurting him, even though it felt like she hurt herself even more. He did not allow her mistake to interfere with his relationship with his budding baby boy, whom he loved with everything in him. He was proud to become the young boy's father. It wasn't easy to walk away from their relationship and end the plans of becoming a family. The fact that they wouldn't wake up to their son together every day anymore was a battle that they fought through, able to co-parent respectfully.

Nicole's mistake caused her character harm when she was labeled a slut by her close relatives and other people who knew or had heard about her mishap with her son's father's friend. They saw her as a loose, fast girl when, really, it was just a mistake she made and never made again. They both moved on with their lives and continued to raise and support their son without distractions.

Level Up

Nicole needed a job. She sought out a position at Whole Foods near her home to support herself and her son. She was hired and worked there for several years. During her time working at Whole Foods, she felt like she had gotten a grip on her life, and wanted more for herself and her son.

She knew she had to start where she left off. The challenge of revisiting her past was necessary to overcome and achieve success for her future. Nicole found that finishing school wasn't as difficult a task as she assumed it would be. Her traumatic past being violated at school gave her a horrible unexplainable feeling to her gut anytime she thought about school. Shortly after becoming a victim of rape, Nicole became numb and remained that way, until she eventually dropped out of high school.

Now that she had a happy, healthy baby boy, she wanted to afford a stable lifestyle, and she knew by going back to school to obtain her diploma was a good start. Nicole enrolled in Ruth Ross Adult Education. It was challenging trying to complete the course while taking care of her child. It was a new challenge for her. To relinquish her parental guidance for a moment was too long for her liking, but she had to do what was necessary.

Nicole's sisters and aunts helped care for her son while she worked and went to school. She was actually more focused this time around than she was during her high school days. Nicole's determination beat all the frustration she previously dealt with from time-to-time. Quality time with her son was never compromised as much as the quantity. That was hard, but achieving her goal was worth it. Nicole graduated in 1991. She was twenty-three years young, and she did it! She was so proud of herself.

The night's highlight was when her name was called by none other than our first lady of Civil Rights and the mother of freedom, Mrs. Rosa Parks. Nicole was moved mostly for the fact that Rosa Parks handed over her diploma, placing it in her hand. She felt honored to walk across that stage, being recognized by such an important woman who imposed a huge impact on all of our lives. Nicole is thankful to Mrs. Rosa Parks for her warm embrace. It is forever treasured and appreciated. With that mega boost of inspiration, she left school ready to set more goals for her life. Her confidence grew with assurance.

She proved to herself that she could achieve more than she thought by never giving up on whatever she dedicated herself to doing. She continued working and parenting while still living with her Aunt Lynn and her sisters in her grandmother's house. This living arrangement continued as they were before Nicole's grandmother, Lurlee, died. They were bonded together as a united front.

In Other Words

The times Nicole needed her mom most were shouldered by her aunts. When Nicole talked about life with her aunts, they would say things or give advice that always seemed like something her mom would have said to her. Florence and her sisters thought a lot alike in some instances. It was nice, but none of it replaced her mom's touch or Nicole's yearning for it. She thought about how proud her mom must feel to have her sisters step in for her when she couldn't be here to care for her own.

Their aunts were already close to their nieces, and cared for them the same while their mom was alive. They were extra protective over their nieces once their sister Florence passed. All of them had their differences at various times with one another, for whatever reason. They all were growing, and some thought they knew everything, so arguments initially ensued amongst the sisters through those measures. There were disagreements that they worked out, and some they just dealt with.

Nicole kept busy working and parenting. She partied when she could. Most times, she partied at home or at a relative's house. She would laugh, listen to music, drink her favorite spirits, and play games, enjoying their time together. Nicole's family visited one another often.

They would see some relatives a few times each week. Grandma Lurlee's house was the go-to place when you were hungry, or just in need of a little love. You were going to get it there, for sure. That tender loving care continued after Mrs. Lurlee Ballard passed. The energy never changed in that house; it was a Ballard thing. Nicole's Aunt Pat lived with them for a while in their grandma's house.

She can't remember why or when her Aunt Pat moved in with them. It had to be of personal reasons because she had another home of her own. Her home was occupied by one of her children, if Nicole remembers correctly. She never asked her why she came to stay, but her Aunt Pat was definitely welcomed. Nicole loved her family and needed them around her more than she liked. She is most grateful for those times, because none of her aunts are alive now, but the memories will be cherished forever. Nicole feels blessed to have had that closeness with her loved ones. If they weren't as close, she would have minimal memories that are priceless and irreplaceable.

Lobbying for a Hobby

Keeping a job was a must for Nicole. She did that faithfully. Nicole worked for a company for over ten years before taking a medical leave of absence that ended her employment there. Before she left that company, Nicole worked and paid all the bills. It was sometimes frustrating to find that some bills had accumulated. If she didn't pay them, she felt they would not have been paid.

No one else in the Ballard family house worked besides Nicole for an extended period of time. Nicole does not complain about this, and she is not sharing this to be disruptive at all. Her only aim is to be as transparent as she will allow herself to be, giving limits in certain areas discussed. Once again, Nicole and her family did everything together. Everyone had a part to play in, which they did. Together, they were complete and did the best that they could.

Nicole wasn't the only parent out of her sisters by this time. Things did start to change, as they all began to have different lives outside of their home. Nicole was either at work or home, on most days of the week.

One evening, Nicole's friend called to invite her out. Nicole accepted the offer, instead of her regular routine of just staying home. It was hard to get her out of the house, but she was open to taking a break from the norm this night. Nicole and her friends met up with some other friends of theirs at a club known for having good music and cute guys that looked like they had plenty of money. This place was perfect for dancing, having fun, and possibly linking up with a fine guy. Nicole felt it must have been her lucky night when she met a guy who appeared to be all she hoped to find.

Nicole and the young man she met that night exchanged phone numbers and talked a few times before they hooked up. After spending some time together, Nicole found herself expecting a child again.

Once Nicole knew for sure that she was pregnant, she called the guy she met at the club that night and dated a few times. She knew it was his child, because she had not been sexually active with anyone else around that time. They weren't in any type of committed relationship, and they had not fallen in love or anything like that. It was casual at best. She did not talk to him on her first attempt, because she couldn't make a connection. He wasn't always available.

He did return her call one day or so later. Nicole had time to think and meditate on her situation by then. She did not get the chance to tell him that she was expecting his child because he quickly mentioned that he is in a relationship with another young lady. This explained to Nicole the reason that their contact with one another was random.

Nicole backed off him, not wanting to interfere with his life, mostly in fear of rejection. Nicole felt too ashamed to tell him she was pregnant. What the two of them had was just a moment. He was dedicated to his girlfriend. Nicole chose to keep the news to herself and leave him alone. She knew she was pregnant a few weeks after being with the father, but never expected this outcome. She felt different in a way that made her fear the possible reality of becoming a mother of two.

She didn't plan on being a mom again, and not so soon. She thought she would've chosen the perfect husband and father before conceiving a child again. Nicole never wanted to terminate her pregnancy or give up her child. She was trying to do better with her life, but her decisionmaking failed her yet again, or so it seemed at that time. She learned from her mistakes not to be a repeater of self-destruction. Her family thought she didn't know who her daughter's father was, because she kept it to herself.

Nicole told her family that she did not want to disclose the information of who the expecting father is for personal reasons. Let's not forget about the incident that ended her relationship with her son's father. That situation falsely characterized Nicole as a slut for many years. Her family was convinced of it by this second conception, especially by way of her secrecy. Nicole blew her family off and kept her secret to herself. The family was supportive of Nicole's pregnancy yet and still. She had help when she needed it, and love and acceptance tried and true. Not sharing that special time and experience with the father, this pregnancy was different and lonely at times. Nicole had a rough time carrying her baby in her final trimester, which ensured that she would be delivering her last child this time.

Say What You Mean and Mean What You Say

Nicole and her sisters received a call from Motown, inviting them to the Sixth Annual Soul Train Music Awards, held at the Shrine Auditorium in Los Angeles, California, March 10, 1992. Nicole knew this would be a challenge for her, because this trip was way too close to her giving birth. She knew this would be the one trip she was not going to make. Meanwhile, Nicole's sisters were planning for this trip and had invited one of their cousins to go in Nicole's place. Yet still, everyone was excited and ready for the birth of Nicole's new baby. Nicole worked all the time, through her pregnancy and up until she went into labor.

While Nicole was in labor, her sisters and cousin were boarding a plane at Detroit Metro Airport headed to Los Angeles, California. This Soul Train Award ceremony was hosted by the late and great Luther Vandross, Will Smith, and Vanessa Williams. Patti Labelle, whom Nicole sends her love to and appreciates for her acts of kindness and concern after losing her mom Florence, did a superb job hosting that night as well. Nicole watched the show from home later when it aired.

Peace and much respect to the late Don Cornelius, who created the nationally syndicated dance and music TV show, *Soul Train*. At age 75, Don Cornelius was found dead at his home in California with an apparent self-inflicted gunshot wound to his head on February 1, 2012. He always ended *Soul Train* with, "We wish you love, peace, and soul!" Right back at you, Mr. Cornelius. A lengthy drama series which airs on the BET Network titled *American Soul* depicts the life and times of Mr. Don Cornelius with great detail.

Nicole's sisters were in attendance, along with one of their female cousins who pretty much went with them most times. Nicole felt it was extremely nice of her Poppa Gordy to cover an additional guest or two to accompany herself and her sisters when they were invited to Motown events local and long-distance. This event was one that Nicole had to sit out. She was faced with an urgent call of duty that required her presence and cooperation in Detroit, Michigan. She was left behind, hospitalized in labor and preparing to deliver her baby girl, whom she named after her mother Florence, of course.

Somehow, Nicole's sisters and cousin ended up with Snoop Dogg after the awards show. Michelle called her while riding with Snoop, rambling on about too much for Nicole to remember. She does remember her sister putting Snoop on the phone after speaking a few unfavorable words to her, knowing she wished she could have been there. Snoop didn't make it any better. He told Nicole, "Wish you were here. Gone shit that baby girl out, baby girl." Nicole replied,

NICOLE

"Fuck you Snoop!" She was so irritated with them, and not to mention the labor pains that were progressing to frequent status at that time. She heard all about the great time they had there.

Nicole missing out wasn't enough for them to just go on and enjoy themselves, without rubbing it in her face every step of the way. They called her the next day with more updates and checked on her, now that the hype had calmed. They were informed that Nicole had her baby girl. Her family shared many funny stories about their time with Snoop and the others that accompanied Snoop. Everyone was cool, and they were perfect gentlemen who treated them like family. It was all love.

On Wednesday, March 11, 1992, Nicole finally gave birth to her much-needed relief. Her aunts were there with her at the hospital throughout her stay. Everyone had advice to give. While one would be smoothing and shaping her daughter Florence's head, another family member would have her involved in a conversation about nursing her new baby girl, wearing Nicole down with all the details of why it was healthier to nurse for herself and the baby. It didn't matter, because Nicole was not with it after giving it a try. The only thing she was thinking was that birthing babies was not her thing. She knew she'd had her last child after having her lovely baby, Florence. If only her mom were alive to witness the birth of her granddaughter.

Nicole had moments to herself, thinking of how things would be if her mom were here with her now. She wonders what Florence would have taught her about parenting. She learned how important it is to protect your children in the most damming way. Daughters and sons need to be guarded against predators of all types. They lurk around you unknowingly, and are related to you in many cases. This was a definite fear of Nicole's. She refused to allow anything to happen to her children.

Having her baby girl gave her life a lift. By the time her baby girl turned fifteen, Nicole had found out that her daughter's dad was single. Since he was not with the young lady he was dating during his and Nicole's moment, she decided to contact and inform him that he had a daughter. Nicole made contact with him, and didn't waste time announcing the news. He was confused and shocked. He asked a few questions, the main one being could he see her.

"Of course," Nicole told him, "That's why I'm telling you about her." They made plans for him to come over to visit his daughter. Now it was time to have a talk with her daughter, to let her know that she would be meeting her father. Nicole also needed to explain why she was told a different story when she was a young girl. Nicole needed her daughter to know the truth right now. It was time for her baby girl to meet her father for the first time.

Nicole's daughter, Florence, was somewhat confused with many blended thoughts. She asked her mom all the questions she could think of about her suddenly unveiled biological father. Nicole answered her daughter truthfully, preparing her for a big day in her life. Florence's dad came as planned.

Their first time seeing one another was an emotional moment. The resemblance was uncanny. It was obvious to all. They had daddy-daughter time talking about any and everything they could think of. Nicole gave them some alone time to speak without a mother's interference. They welcomed each other, and he has loved his daughter from that moment on. They have a beautiful father-daughter relationship. Nicole's daughter is the light of her life. It was hard for her to believe she was a mother of two. She had help from her family, who was always there for her. When Nicole became frustrated with parenting and needed a break, as most single parents do sometimes, they were there to relieve her. She is forever grateful for her family's love and support. It will never be forgotten. She thanked them for that and loved them to pieces always. Nicole was a mother before anything else, and spent her time trying to be the best mom she knew how to be.

Change Gone Come

    Meanwhile, another life-changing experience in the Ballard household was nearing full speed ahead at 18273 Glastonbury Street, which held the Ballard family together, sheltering three generations in that home. It was home to many at one point in time when Nicole's grandmother Lurlee Ballard was living. Not much of that changed after her grandmother died. That home was like a refuge to some and a revolving door for others, holding more memories than any other house that Nicole's ever lived in.

    She remembers her Uncle Gilbert, whom the family called Gibby. Uncle Gibby was a bright light every time he came around. He played with our children and was a good uncle to all of his nieces and nephews. Uncle Gibby stopped by the Ballard home to drop off a chicken bucket for the household at least once a week. They also called Gibby their chicken man. It was disheartening when they received the call notifying them of Gibby's passing in 1994. Nicole knew she had to be strong and carry on. It was sad, and it did cause some depression, but working and caring for her two children helped keep her from being in a state of depression far too long. Nicole became the responsible one, as far as paying all of the household bills. She worked hard to keep things up for everyone's comfort. This was the summons of her burden. Not being equipped with the tools to survive the unknown, she thought she did well enough to keep what they had. Receiving unexpected mail did not get much attention, if it got opened at all.

    Nicole did not understand the level of destruction that was brewing. It was apparent to Nicole that if you miss payments on your home, you get put out. She knew it was different with ownership, because she missed a few payments, and nothing happened. A few letters came in the mail before it became a faint priority. She believed that one of her aunts knew the severity of their housing delinquency, if not both, because someone had to see the tax papers even if they didn't understand them. Nicole did not know much about homeownership, besides the obvious: to pay the monthly mortgage payments.

She can't say who ultimately dropped the ball, so she declares that they all collectively failed that mission. Everyone contributed in various ways. They just didn't have a dedicated system to dictate who was responsible for what, specifically. Homeowner's taxes were something Nicole didn't know anything about, either. She felt like she was in charge, since no one else was fighting to be. Together they lost the house Florence bought for her mother. It was devastating and humiliating. It hurt like she could never explain, but they eventually were able to move on with their lives. Their Aunt Pat went back to her house, and their Aunt Lynn moved with Nicole, Michelle, Lisa, and their children until Michelle and Lisa moved out on their own.

This was when Nicole learned to appreciate alone time. Once her babies were sleeping, Nicole would practice meditation to help deal with her internal pain. Giving more time to think freely always leads her into the thoughts of her deepest hurt, a place where she would allow herself to relive the moments in her mind. Nicole would often drink a beer or more to mask the pain she felt once certain thoughts would pop up in her head. There were many tearful nights thinking about some of the things that happened to her in her life after her mom passed, how they maybe would not have happened had her mother remained alive.

Nicole was a proud mom. Her daughter was growing up fast right before her eyes. It didn't seem like a full twelve months before another birthday would come. Nicole began to meditate on birthday party ideas for her daughter Florence who was, and still is, Nicole's baby doll. While thinking of ideas for her daughter, she drifted off into thinking back on hers and her sister's last birthday with their mom, and how amazing it was. Their Aunt Pat and Maxine helped their mom Florence decorate the house and prepare the food. Nicole's Aunt Lynn showed up with the cakes, but she and Michelle could not see it yet. Florence made sure to dress her twins beautifully. She liked to dress them alike. Nicole remembers the way she felt on that day. She felt special and very pretty. Once the party began, they were brought outside to the backyard for their special, surprise introductory.

The twins had no idea what was going on, but they were excited to find out. Florence walked her twin daughters outside to the backyard area and stopped them at a table where their cakes rested.

The cakes were so beautiful that Nicole and Michelle's eyes lit up. They were so pleased with their exquisite tiered cake. Each cake was personalized with their names and age. The cakes were fancy and dressed like a wedding cake. When Nicole looked up and away from her cake, her mom started her announcement. Florence asked for everyone's undivided attention as she welcomed and introduced The Emotions.

Florence's special birthday gift to her daughters was a private performance from The Emotions singing their hit single, "Best of My Love," to her darling twins in front of friends and family. It was quite the birthday party. Nicole didn't grasp how big of a deal that really was then. It wasn't uncommon to have different celebrities around sometimes, especially during holidays and other celebrations. Turning seven years old felt great. October 13, 1975, marked Florence's last birthday celebration for and with her twins. No other birthdays ever mattered to Nicole since that one.

One thing Nicole does not recall about her seventh birthday party is seeing her dad there. She cannot remember seeing Tommy any that day, before, during, or after the party. She feels like he was not there at all. It was not noticed at the time, but it is definitely understood today.

Recognizing Flo' After Death

On November 10, 2001, Nicole and her sisters were invited to The Pioneer Awards held at The Apollo Theatre in Harlem, New York. The Ballard daughters were special guests. Nicole and Michelle received a call from Mr. Gordy Jr.'s assistant, who called to notify the girls of the event planned. Michelle is and has always been the main receiver of contact with everyone from Motown. Nicole doesn't remember the exact date that the assistant contacted them, but she does remember it all taking place soon after the unforgettable 9/11 tragedy. Receiving that phone call at a tragic time like that felt necessary and warm.

Nicole was informed that her mother, Florence Ballard Chapman, would be honored with an award at the event. Wow, about time! was probably Nicole's first thought. She became instantly emotional. The assistant went on to say, "Not only are you all arriving as special guests, but you will also be accepting your mom's award!"

This was the best feeling ever for Nicole. She almost felt vindicated in some way, but not totally. The feeling felt more like the honoring of her mother Florence was long overdue, so accepting that invitation was easy and gratefully so. The girls gave two of their cousins' information, notifying that they would travel with them. The assistant to Motown said she would call them back with a detailed itinerary within a few days. The assistant did call back with their flight information and other notable details, but it was mainly time to pack. Nicole talked about this happening for days before it got old. She told all of her family and some friends all about the big day planned to recognize her mom with honor, and she could not wait for that day to come.

She watched a lot of New York news to keep track of the 9/11 attack developments, the stability, adjustments, and weather as it applied to the preparation of their upcoming visit. It was hard to focus on their exciting news without discussing the massive loss of life and massive landmark structures. Every conversation was led with newfound discoveries.

Peace and Blessings

It was devastating knowing that some people weren't recovered from the debris after the implosive terrorist attack on New York's most toured landmarks. They were concerned about the outcome of New York's tragedy, and if things would be restored by the time of their planned arrival. Nicole had no idea it would take as long as it did to finalize the restoration of the disastrous area and locate all the missing Americans lost in the rubble. Two-thousand-seven hundred-fifty-three people died that day. One-thousand-one-hundred-thirteen had yet to be identified. No trace of them was found. The total absence of remains, and any other physical evidence of their being, had to be an unimaginable feeling for those dear to these untraceable victims. This certainly touched the hearts of the United States as a people.

Nicole's emotions were high at moments, feeling much grief and sorrow for the major loss. She didn't know how she would feel stepping on the soil that so recently received such an unbelievable tragedy. The images and thoughts never vacated her mind as they headed to the airport. The girls and their guests were flown on a small plane, not to mistake it for a private jet, but small, as in, the smallest

Nicole had ever flown on. Small enough to catch every wind-wave taking her breath away each and every time. The turbulence made it feel smaller than it was. Thanks to alcoholic beverages.; Nicole was able to subdue her fears to make it through the flight. There were other passengers on this flight, to the sum of maybe twenty people. These people were too comfortable on this flight for Nicole. Everyone caught a wind wave or two with gasping outbursts, but no one seemed as concerned as she was herself. The turbulence was not familiar to Nicole, which made her feel it had much to do with the aircraft's size. Nicole was praying to make it to New York safely.

Once those little wheels stopped rolling, Nicole was ready to exit the plane after it felt like the weather had slapped it upside down. "It felt like a fight with Mother Nature," Nicole explained. She was eternally thankful to Mother Nature for releasing them to land without injury. Nicole was more than ready to exit the plane, which always takes too long, testing her patience. Nicole can be somewhat irrational in a situation of this sort. She hates the moment when the plane is parked, but you can't get up yet. She gets impatient on airplanes and in airports—too many restrictions after an extremely turbulent flight. Even with full understanding that the restrictions are put in place for safety reasons, it's still frustrating.

Their arrival in New York was chaotic. They were anxious, nervous, and excited all at the same time. Everyone wanted to be the one in charge, knowing everything and lead the pack. After a few back and forth, they collectively decided to listen to the one with the papers, instead of the one who wanted us to trust their memory. Total chaos, but they ended up in the right area at the right time.

They found their ride/driver, who was a handsome gentleman. It may be more appropriate to say the driver found them. He recognized the girls, as he was probably prepped to do so. After all the bickering and disagreements going on, they had to appear lost and confused, except for the leader, who will remain nameless, but they knew everything and walked off, as if she had been there before. They all agreed with her this time, because she held the blueprint in her hand and led them to their destination from start to finish without incident. Although the flight was rough and their arrival was hectic, things moved like clockwork, and fast-paced thankfully. There were two immediate feelings they felt stepping on the grounds of New York; the obvious one was excitement, and the other was how cold it was there.

Nicole didn't expect it to be colder than it was back at home in Michigan. She thought her mother must have been accustomed to the cold growing up in Detroit, Michigan, to have moved to New York, where the winter weather was colder than Michigan. This was Nicole's first time in New York. It seemed like everyone there was in a hurry as if there was a constant emergency on high alert. With the fresh residue of 9/11 present, Nicole's frequency levels were fluctuating rapidly. Nicole was excited, but the energy made her sad, and she was colder than if she'd had the flu. She almost felt warped into that time and moment. The energy was strongly magnetic. To put it short, she felt a connection with the lost. The emotional part of magnetic energy was draining, and the frequent battles with herself trying to shut down the connection. It was overbearing, and caused her mood to shift uncontrollably.

That was a lot for a short, patient and tempered Nicole. She is someone who can only take so much before she starts voicing her opinions, with little concern for the receiver. Nicole's other issue was her feet were hurting. She wore the wrong boots. They were not made for walking.

The minute she decided to sit down and let them find the driver, he appeared as the doors nearest them opened. He was holding a sign that said, *Ballard*. "Just a few more steps and I will be okay," is all Nicole kept repeating to herself, although she did notice that he was fine as wine. Of course, she tried to walk as straight as possible so not to look silly upon their first acquaintance. They quickly approached him after Michelle, and the driver made eye contact and confirmed with a head nod that they were in fact, the Ballards that he was looking for. Now everybody's trying to look cute for the driver. All the ladies' walk and tone of voice changed. It is hilarious thinking about it today. Nicole wouldn't tell everything that happened with the fine driver and their stay, because she vowed to keep some things a secret.

They could not reach the car fast enough. As they approached the driver, he first introduced himself to them. Nicole cannot remember his name at all, so we will continue addressing him as Mr. Fine. Everyone was standing at the car now with their bags when Mr. Fine asked them to drop their bags, then gestured them to the car and opened the limo's door. They got inside and made themselves comfortable. He walked to the back of the limo, where their bags were left to put them in the trunk. Nicole was so happy to be off of her feet and in from the cold frigid air. She noticed a tray of drinks behind them as they sat in the car while the driver loaded up their luggage. Once he entered the driver's side door, they couldn't see him until a small window partition opened, and he began speaking as if from a script. He was hired to be their escort throughout the entire stay. He mentioned the drinks behind them were complimentary, and that was all they needed to hear. Nicole was sure the others were just as ready to unwind as she was. They did not hesitate to make drinks while he continued with the script. He mentioned that he would be their refuge in any and all situations.

He was the go-to and the go-between guy. What service he did not offer, he would supply them with someone who could meet their needs. He was at their every beck and call. Nicole and her sisters were linked to him via cellphone. They also had passwords/codes for certain situations and in case of emergencies. He was honored to meet and assist Florence Ballard's kids, connected to one of Motown's highest moments in music history.

Mr. Fine made a call, then began to drive off. They were getting a little loud, trying to get a drink in everyone's hand with the attempt to warm up expeditiously. They never missed an opportunity to be amateur comedians or just plain silly. The Ballard family loved to laugh and crack jokes on each other. It felt so good for Nicole to be off her feet and unwind for a moment. They all were warming up and sipping on spirits of choice as the excitement returned, replacing Nicole's anxiety and frustration. They laughed so much while having a really good time forgetting about everything left behind in their hometown in Detroit, the Motor City.

Mr. Fine mentioned in his speech that their first stop would be the hotel unless anyone had a request. No one did, so the driver proceeded on to their temporary residence. The ride was smooth and enlightening, catching a glimpse of New York here and there while looking out of the window in between conversations with everyone. Nicole found herself constantly grateful for the car service thinking of New York's transit systems, especially at that time, while things were not operating to the fullest accessibility. Everyone was late to where they were headed, is how it seemed, no matter what time of day or night. That cold weather would make a turtle move fast.

After about thirty minutes of driving, they arrived at the Waldorf Astoria Hotel. They had never been treated less than V.I.P. status by Mr. Berry Gordy Jr., but to them, it felt even bigger every time no matter where they were invited. If you are not familiar with The Waldorf Astoria New York Hotel, the design and decorative spread was pure D'Elegance. The appeal was Class A. The energy and presence of the staff were prestigious and welcoming.

Mr. Fine assisted them all inside the hotel and organized their luggage with the concierge. He then made a call to someone, saying, "We made it." Nicole and the others checked into their room, a corner suite with two bedrooms opposite the central living room space. The room was reserved with an amazing view near the top floor. They were comfortably spread out within the maybe six-hundred square feet or more of space. They only had an hour to get dressed to arrive at the venue on time. Their luggage arrived at their room shortly after they checked in.

Mr. Fine told them that he would be outside waiting for them. They got themselves together and made it to the venue before the honorary celebration started. They took their seats after speaking to a few people who knew them. Mr. Fine entered with them as well. There were moments when some people asked who Nicole and her sisters were, or gave hesitation to accepting their presence until they were informed of who they were by other celebrities in the building. They were all smiles once they were aware of Nicole and her company's identities. This was a pet peeve of Nicole's that happened too many times that night. Being prejudged is insulting. It's sad how most of them see nothing wrong with being this way.

Before they could meet the loving Nicole, they triggered the bitchy Nicole, who is sensitive and defensive. Bitchy Nicole will let you know if she's not pleased with your actions. She has no tolerance for poor social ethics directed towards her. Nicole is almost certain that her face said what her mouth did not need to say. She was trying to live in the moment, while ignoring the ignorance.

Nicole took a deep breath and turned her attention back to the show, patiently waiting for the announcement that brought her there. Berry Gordy put the event together to honor and celebrate the extraordinary talent that had surrounded him for decades on end. These gifted artists were well-deserving of an elevated level of recognition and appreciation. Holland Dozier and Holland were honored, and they were surprised to have been mentioned in such honor. Not that they did not think they deserved it; it was just out of nowhere, and after so much time had elapsed with nothing being done or said publicly. They kindly accepted.

These awards come with monetary gift attachments. The title determines the amount. Al Green was honored but did not attend. It was explained that the once-secular musician, turned gospel artist and reverend, was elsewhere, ministering to a church member. Mr. Al Green gifted his attached $20,000 award back to Motown. His decisions were well respected. Sly and the Family Stone were honored and performed, minus Sly himself. Sly had been living a secluded lifestyle for decades before the award show. The gifted lead singer, writer, and music producer of this group were not expected to show up as much as the hope that he would be projected. The recent death of Mr. Sly Stone's father, paired with the September 11th attack, diminished his ability to celebrate. His family spoke for him at the end of their performance saying, "Sly was elated to be honored and most appreciative that fans are still listening to his music with interest in him and his talent."

Now finally, the moment Nicole had been waiting for. They started with Diana Ross. Nicole clapped for Diana when her daughter Rhonda went up to accept her award. They all clapped for Mary Wilson also, as her daughter accepted her award. Once everyone was seated, Nicole and her sisters waited for their mom, Florence Ballard's name to be called, but it didn't happen. Nicole became a little perturbed when she noticed the miss in the announcement. Her sister Michelle noticed Nicole's reaction to this, and began to ask Nicole not to start anything with the Motown family. At that very moment, Nicole tossed her drink in her sister Michelle's face out of frustration. Yes, her drink was all in Michelle's eyes. She was upset about it, no doubt, but held her composure as best she could. Her makeup and eyelashes were her main concern.

Freddie Jackson was seated a few seats away. He saw and heard it all. He felt comfortable enough to lean in and asked, "Are you girls alright?" Nicole replied, "Shut up Freddie!" He backed off immediately. It was becoming apparent that the girls noticed the miss in honoring their mom Florence, hearing things heat up in their seating area. Mr. Fine was instructed to inform the Ballard daughters of the mishap. They were told that their mom's award was not there, but it did exist. Nicole couldn't believe they had left out or forgotten her mom's award, of all people. This was when the drama began. Nicole left the event to calm her sisters, but she was definitely returning to set things straight with Motown and whoever was responsible for forgetting her mom's award. That one mistake turned Nicole's night upside down.

Michelle begged Nicole not to go back with that attitude, but it was too late. Nicole had one thing and one thing only on her agenda, so the girls went to bed while Nicole headed back out to the after party. She entered with an attitude and was ready for all and any confrontations. She saw Mary Wilson's award, so she took it and left with it. Nicole received calls about Mary Wilson's award. They pleaded with Nicole to return Mary's award back to her, but Nicole refused to comply. It did not matter who called; Nicole did not budge in any way, shape, or form. She told them, "When y'all produce my mom's award, Aunt Mary can get hers back." Mary Wilson and Nicole made plans to meet up outside of Bert's Wearhouse, downtown Detroit about a week or so later to exchange awards. Mary arrived with Florence's award in hand. Mary smiled and hugged her as she understood Nicole's grief. It was all forgiven.

Nicole wasn't proud of her actions as much as she wasn't proud of theirs. Forgetting her mom's award was like a slap in the face to her children and family. Forgetting can easily be taken as carelessness or neglect. It was insulting and offensive. People love to fill you up with kind words and sympathy, with no real action or intent. In this case, the action finally happened, but it was diminished by neglect.

In Nicole's mind, that moment was mapped out. She was accepting her mother's award, and she had some things to say. She had every intention of being positive and kind, but things went left quickly, and all of a sudden. Nicole's take on the situation was well understood by all. If anyone were to react in such a way, it would be expected of her.

Love and Support to the Max

Nicole's Aunt Maxine was the smartest lady she knew. Her Aunt Max had all the answers. She taught her nieces many values in life and always supported them in whatever they chose to do. Church and faith in God were very important to Maxine for herself and her family. Maxine was a nonstop achiever. Whatever she desired to do, whether it was a temporary idea or a long term one, she would see it through. Nicole will never forget the bond they shared, leaving many memories to cherish. Maxine lived 71 years of a full life before departing on December 13, 2013.

The Book Max Wrote

Nicole feels her Aunt Maxine's book was full of her truth mixed with self-absorbed judgment and emotions. Nicole can't contest nor attest to much said in the pre-existing book, or before her existence. Nicole gives her aunt credit, since she was there to witness what Nicole didn't and couldn't for herself. In her book, some accusations Maxine wrote resulted from her sister Florence's emotions and complaints against her husband Tommy after a fallout, a disagreement or an argument with Motown or anyone else.

Florence did not get a chance to resolve some of those issues, which could have resulted in a different outcome today. After Florence left Motown, there were unsettled differences that stretched out over some odd years. Florence's differences were absorbed by her siblings, especially, but not excluding other family members. At the same time, there was a clear understanding that Motown was a business built by a stern, driven alpha male, not to be mistaken. Florence made the decision to walk away. She soon became a married mother of two and was happy with that. Florence's fans were the compelling factor in convincing her to return to the spotlight.

Aunt Pat

Pat played her role as an aunt and stand-in mom to Nicole and her sisters. Nicole's Aunt Pat was there for all of her dimensional periods in life growing up as a preteen, teen, and adult. She was not the easiest to deal with, but at the same time, she was, because of Nicole's nurturing ways. She knows she frustrated her aunts and other family members at times when she would shut down and close everyone out, or when she would explode after reaching her limit. They didn't push too hard when they saw Nicole in that state of mind. They knew she just needed a minute to herself. There were times when Nicole would lose her way and get off track thinking about the inconsistencies in her life that she could not control. She was silent, distant, and emotional at times. Later, she found that talking actually helped. So, she exercised talking more.

Nicole would speak to her aunts about her mom, and they would always feed their niece with all she needed to mask the pain for a while, sometimes ending in laughter and sometimes in tears. They shared stories of their sisterhood with Florence and all the things that mattered in life. Florence and her sisters were close, and did everything together. There was a time when Nicole learned how her mother, Florence, was a rebel, and was all about equal rights. How they were there for the march that Martin Luther King Jr. organized in Detroit, Michigan, down Woodward Avenue during the Civil Rights campaign. They lived in a segregated time, and endured the harsh tones demonstrated against people of color.

Blacks or Negros (as some will call them), all represent a separation that led to the Civil Rights Movement. Nicole's aunts would share how life shifted during the fourteen years of fighting for civil rights, and how the win wasn't much of a win. They taught their nieces how to recognize the modernized slave mentality, and hoped they were equipped with the tools to overcome some or more of the hurdles set up to stop them.

Pat and Lynn were dedicated to their nieces, and vowed never to let Florence down. They were a tight unit, as they were when Florence was alive. Nicole's Aunt Pat was diagnosed with breast cancer. This was devastating to the family, as you may imagine. Aunt Pat was strong and refused to be defeated. She fought and was determined to win. Nicole cared for her aunt and kept her spirits up. It was frustrating for her to become dependent, having to rely on someone to assist or completely do for her what he once did for herself a short time ago. Nicole never allowed her aunt to feel she was burdened by any of her needs. It seemed their prayers were being answered when her Aunt Pat began to heal more each day, until they thought she beat it.

Without a doctor's evaluation, they assumed she was well and in remission. It didn't take long for the cancer cells to return, spreading rapidly. So much so, it had become unmanageable, and they could not keep up because, this time, it spread from one area to the next. On May 8, 2015, the cancer won. Aunt Pat was dead two days before Mother's Day. To this very day, there isn't a moment Nicole regrets or would change when it comes to caring for her aunts in their time of need due to their sudden illnesses. Everyone needs someone sometime in life. She is pleased to have done her part, and hopes she's as lucky to receive the same in return from whoever has it in their heart of hearts to give it to her.

Listen, Linda

Florence's baby sister, Linda K. Ballard, was Nicole's heart. Not that she loved either of her aunts more than the other, it's just a feeling that fills her up when she thinks of her times with Lynn. Nicole shared a synonymously unique bond with each of her aunts that helped fill the void of not having her mother's love present in the physical form. Aunt Lynn never judged Nicole for anything she did. She made many mistakes and ravaged sporadic and reckless behavior for a nice period of time. Aunt Lynn was there for it all, being supportive and understanding. Nicole soon found that it was time to support Lynn.

When Nicole's Aunt Lynn fell ill, it was all of a sudden and undoubtedly serious. Lynn was not a regular visitor of anyone's doctor's office, which would have been the ideal aid in health repair given an early diagnosis, except that was not what Lynn wanted. Nicole witnessed enough medical emergencies by then to recognize and distinguish what "seems" serious versus what "is not." Nicole saw that they were dealing with a severe internal illness. Nothing Nicole said to her Aunt Lynn would make her agree to receiving medical attention. She would not allow Nicole to call any type of emergency respondents at any point in time. Aunt Lynn said she was going to ride this out, like everything else. She was strong and never whimpered. Nicole cared for her aunt every need along with family, from the start of it all, which turned out to be cancer. Nicole's Aunt Lynn died on July 25, 2007, five days after her 54th birthday.

By the time the family addressed the disease, it was terminal. There was no turning it around and no chance for remission, although they were oblivious to these facts at the time. The family of caregivers took turns, giving prompt attention to Lynn each day without taking one moment for granted. The only time Nicole was away was when she had to work. Nicole watched her aunt fade away in a short amount of time. She is ever so grateful for the time they spent together. They shared so much of their inner thoughts that they felt mattered most at the time.

Nicole often pondered the medicating methods the family practiced on her Aunt Lynn, wondering if they were helping or hurting her. It's what she wanted, so the family complied with her wishes that were more like demands. On Lynn's final day of suffering, Nicole sat by her bedside, and together they listened to the radio. Oftentimes, Nicole's mind would venture off into thinking about how her aunt must be feeling. She could never imagine her pain, no matter how much of it she witnessed. Her Aunt Lynn kept her spirits up, never complaining about much of anything. She didn't want to show any signs of weakness until the end. Nicole made sure her Aunt Lynn stayed clean, feed, and medicated. She had a systematic routine that she carried out faithfully, daily. Nicole's sisters helped out, and her other aunts came to spend time with her as they rotated shifts. They did their best with what they then understood.

For a moment, Aunt Lynn has whispered away from all thoughts upon hearing Rihanna's song, "Umbrella," come on. Nicole and her Aunt Lynn started singing it to and with each other. They absolutely loved that song. Suddenly, her Aunt Lynn smiled and said in a happy, strong, clear voice, "I knew at the end, she was going to be here." She grabbed Nicole's hand, kind of soft and slow, but direct and matter-of-fact. It caught Nicole's attention, which took her eyes toward the window where Nicole saw a rainbow coming across their house. She smiled and did not know why. It just felt lovely at this moment.

Nicole brought her attention back to her Aunt Lynn when she said, "Your blessings will start and never stop." Nicole smiled and began to feel immensely saddened at the same time. Instantly, Nicole realized that her aunt had just taken her last breath. Nicole kissed her Aunt Lynn on the lips, then all that happy feeling they were just sharing depleted immediately, transforming into devastation which took control of her emotions. Nicole's sister came into the room behind her as soon as she heard Nicole crying. Nicole felt her sister lean over her shoulder before hugging her for comfort. It was the beginning of another episode of a lost loved one, on such a beautiful day.

Aunt Lynn had two daughters, Brandy and Jessica Ballard, who passed away sometime around and between 2008 and 2010. Almost immediately after their mother died, they did also, one after the other. With some help, Nicole was able to bury her cousin Brandy, but she could not collect enough money to do the same for Jessica. She was able to have a memorial service and had Jessica cremated, which hurt her so badly. She truly wanted to do more, and would have if she could. Nicole's two cousins, Brandy and Jessica, were overweight and had health issues due to obesity. Nicole did try to encourage them to eat better and do better over time, but it was not effective. She doesn't think any of them thought they would actually die anytime soon.

At least Nicole didn't. She was more concerned with life-altering diseases that would cause death later on in life if not treated or addressed properly. Brandy and Jessica were in their early thirties when they died. It hurt Nicole that she could not help them. She's sure there was more she could have done, and maybe should have, but she did what her abilities allowed, and she has to live with that.

Assumptions

As a young adult, Nicole remembers reading the stories about her mom losing her home and living with her Aunt Max for a short period of time until her mother Florence could get back on her feet. It was true to an extent, but it was not as long as it's been insinuated. Nicole was able to remember a time when they stayed at Nicole's Aunt Maxine's home for a short time. To Nicole, it felt like an extended slumber party. One that didn't end when they woke up after the first night. Staying over at each other's homes was so common that this arrangement didn't last long enough to represent a severe situation to a child Nicole's age.

Poverty was never evident to Nicole growing up, although there was a time when she recognized her mother in an uncomfortable and vulnerable state. Later in life, Nicole reassessed that moment in their lives and could then understand the rumor. It just was not like it was told. Her mother was never penniless. Florence had a moment of despair that she did not allow to linger too long. There may have been welfare assistance, but that was only for a moment until it was no longer needed. Florence was not too proud to do what she had to for the benefit of her children. Losing her home, which was her prized possession, took a toll on her, along with her failing marriage to make matters worse.

Florence was dealing with the changes in her life, but she did not allow her children to suffer. A child receiving the appropriate amount of love and attention, blanketed with the bare necessities needed to sustain a decent life, wouldn't allow for one to feel impoverished. Life was good for Nicole. As time and technology progressed, interest in learning more about her mother's life and death became more easily accessible.

Mental Health

At one point in Florence's life, she was falling apart mentally. Most of what was said checked out by admission from family members, and some make sense. Nicole was able to put together the pieces to the puzzle that perplexed her for so long. This must have been a time when Florence had transitioned to a space of feeling unsafe, which led her to eventually seek help.

Nicole remembers the moment of this residential change. Florence told her daughters that they had to move out of their home and find a new house. What all was said, exactly, is like a blur to Nicole today, but she can remember her mother saying they had to move, and were going to find a new house. It was a sad hour, but that did not last long because it was understood. The time spent at Maxine's home was fun, loving, and forever cherished, but there was a void with Nicole at times for not having her own room and space. Before that void could set in good, Florence kept her word, and they were moving out of her sister Maxine's house and into their own home again. That time in total is one that Nicole would only be able to guesstimate. Nicole felt everything happened just like her mom Florence said, and without taking a long time.

It would be fair to assume that Florence would become bothered, if you will, by the progression of the sensational female singing group she once claimed as her own. She was no longer a part of a group's success she constructed, paired with her solo career flopping and troubled marriage, a lethal concoction. Florence's family and friends all agreed that she wanted to live, and was full of anticipation of her new endeavors ahead. Florence was not suicidal, although there were times when she felt like giving up. Florence surrendered to her needs, and began her residency at Henry Ford Hospital Rehabilitation. Florence thought that she could take a minute to escape the pain that haunted her until her death. She found that she needed more than a minute to get back on track. She took this time to soul search. Her sister Maxine had her back with keeping her daughters while Florence took the time to find herself.

Being confused, frustrated, angry, and unemployed can easily segue into depression, aggression, defeat, and emptiness. She was constantly facing adversities. Florence and her sisters Maxine and Pat had many heart-to-heart talks. Florence always spoke truthfully with whomever she engaged in conversation with. Nicole had heard many of her mother's conversations with her sisters. Florence was not concerned with being right as much as she just wanted to be heard. Florence just wanted to pinpoint the problems to fix them better.

The talks amongst the sisters were always displayed with so much passion. Nicole heard enough of them to now understand what her mother was going through and why she started feeling out of place everywhere. Florence did therapy to discuss the things that she didn't understand, and to help her mentally accept some of the failing arrangements encompassing her. She was having a hard time dealing with the new and sudden changes enforced upon her. Music was her life, which eventually left her feeling unfulfilled. She had so much more to share, and she tried in every way to produce more music to be released. Florence was trying to prove her solo artistry was worthy enough to gain a new spot in Hollywood. Reclaim the fame, that was her aim. We all know it didn't happen as she desired. After some therapy, Florence began to turn things around for herself. Florence's mother talked to her often around this time in despair, telling her daughter, "It's not over for you if you don't want it to be." She told Florence that she could still achieve anything because she was a force to be reckoned with.

Throughout that time in Florence's life, there was always Tommy, reappearing at random. He came around here and there to see about his broken family. His main concern was his broken wife undoubtedly. Tommy and Florence split up, but they kept in touch throughout the separation. Tommy knew all that Florence was dealing with. He seemed empathetic and concerned for his wife at times, but did not know how to love her properly.

They were very much in love, just toxic for one another. There was no real tension between Tommy and Nicole's Aunt Maxine when he visited his family. Tommy was welcomed there, even if they felt the need to just grin and bear it at times. They expressed their dislike for Tommy more so when he and Florence would fight. It's natural for a family to express that type of reaction out of concern for their loved one's safety. Most times, this reaction is questionable due to the fact that most couples end up back together, usually every time until there are no more times. No one ever knows when that time is up. It just happens, then after a while, we recognize it and claim it. That's when we know it's over. Well, it wasn't quite over for Florence and Tommy Chapman yet, but this would be the last time they united after a separation. Florence successfully completed her stay in rehabilitation and was released. After rehabilitation, Florence initiated a new attitude and outlook on life.

Love Ain't Love

Florence gained her confidence back and began a new plan for the future of hers and her family. This plan would allow her to drop the welfare assistance. Nicole is not sure about the replaced source of income, but Florence bought a new 878 square foot house, built-in 1947, located at 17071 Shaftsbury Avenue in Detroit, Michigan. Shortly after, Tommy returned to be back home with his family. This home would be a lot smaller than the house she bought before she became a mom. It was the same size as the home she had previously bought for her mother on Glastonbury Avenue. The two homes were also built the same year. The neighborhood was decent then, and occupied by homeowners.

Florence also bought her and Tommy both new cars. Matching Cadillac Sevilles. Florence drove a blue Cadillac, while her husband Tommy was gifted a black one. Nicole remembers her father, Tommy, coming home from work with gifts for her and her sisters like every few days, it seemed. One day he bought the girls a baby-living type doll that they would see on TV, and wanted. It was like a real baby. Nicole can't remember all the things he bought in specifics, but it happened enough to make a kid feel special.

Although Nicole felt spoiled, she didn't feel it in a sense of wealth. She never felt rich or anything like that. It was more like love, when your parents get you pretty much all that you ask for type of spoiling. Nicole watched her dad shower her mom with gifts as well. Florence was mostly interested in her children having a loving, complete Christmas holiday. She wanted things to be alright and look that way. She tried all that she could think to make her marriage work before deciding to end it. Things were back on track, and everything was great for a few months, before it would ultimately end for good.

Where Did the Money Go?

There have been concerned fans of Florence on different blog sites that have questioned what happened to the money that Nicole and her sisters were rumored to have received from Diana Ross and other assumed names. The rumors were not accurate, but held some truth.

There was a time or two when Nicole's Uncle Billie obtained some portions of Motown's financial contributions, and used them for his benefit. Nicole and her sisters were too young to intervene at the time, and we were not privy to the details until after it happened. Her uncle must have needed it, and she felt that it was not malicious.

Her Aunt Lynn bought a car with money that was sent for Nicole and her sisters. Lynn absolutely needed a car. It was a necessary purchase that helped Nicole's grandmother get around as well as herself and her sisters. But first, Lynn gave Nicole and her sisters

$500 each, out of the money to do whatever they chose. They went to Northland Shopping Mall, which is a popular landmark in Detroit, Michigan. Lynn had become the primary guardian over Nicole and her sisters, making decisions on their behalf once her mother, Lurlee, fell ill with cancer twice before passing on. Lynn always had the help of all of her siblings, who loved Florence's daughters as well. Everyone played their part in caring for Nicole, Michelle, and Lisa, doing the best that they could.

CHAPTER CUATRO

SETTING THE RECORD STRAIGHT

Broken Leg

Pan-African News Wire and its editor, Abayomi Azikiwe, released and published an article on December 30, 2006, making these statements below, which are incorrect.

"Below we are reprinting factual information on the life of Florence Ballard (1943-1976), who is credited with forming the original group, The Primettes, which later became the Supremes. In 1975, Ballard received a settlement from a slip-and-fall incident in which she had broken her leg after slipping on a patch of ice in Detroit."

The link to this article:
http://panafricannews.blogspot.com/2006/12/florence-ballard-life-behind dreamgirls_30.html?m=1

Another story was that Tommy did it somehow, possibly by causing Florence to fall down the stairs in their home. While Tommy was abusive to Florence, Nicole says, "That did not happen!" None of the rumored stories are true. Florence broke her leg simply by tripping over her nephew, who was sleeping over with her daughters and other family members on the living room floor. Nicole's cousins, especially Chris, loved being around their Aunt Florence.

All the kids were quiet and resting. Maybe a total of five or six kids spread out within the front room of the house having a sleepover. It was dark when Florence decided to tiptoe around the sleeping children and tripped. There were screams and yells of shock and maybe some pain, but Florence masked it by actually laughing at herself after making sure she didn't hurt her nephew. The severity of Florence's injury was quite a shock to them all. Tommy came quickly and turned the lights on.

They all knew it was more serious than Florence had led on by laughing and worrying more about the kids than herself by the way she couldn't get up. Florence was in pain, but she didn't cry. Once Tommy had to assist her in getting up is when it gradually began to look more serious. Florence made some faces and sounds that indicated pain, but it seemed tolerable. The hospital visit and cast confirmed just how serious that simple accident turned out to be.

We all could speculate that Florence could have received a settlement from her homeowner's insurance for her injury, but it would be just that: pure speculation. Nicole knows now that her mother received funds before the leg injury that can be attached to Motown one way or another. She won't say how much or how often it would be too much to disclose. Most of it is already written here in this book. The timeline will help you figure out what's available to be understood.

Urban Legend

Diana Ross was not welcome to Florence Ballard Chapman's funeral, and she did not attend Florence's burial.

Correction

Diana Ross was more than welcomed and expected. Fans were booing her, and the family didn't understand why they were against Diana so strongly while the family was welcoming her with open arms. The Ballard family has always loved Diana. Diana did not try to upstage Florence at her funeral, like some people were suggesting. Diana only did what she knew how to do. In moments of sorrow, it's hard to plan things out the way you would have liked to, had you been better prepared. You don't get enough time to mourn and plan your words and actions within a short period of time.

Nicole and her sisters grew up calling Diana Auntie Boss, and never Diana. She was always there for Florence's daughters. Diana never missed a birthday, or Christmas for the girls. If she ever missed one, Nicole didn't notice it. There was a time when Diana sent Nicole and her sisters fur coats. Beautiful Mink jackets. They were so excited and appreciative. The girls couldn't wait to wear their new fur coats, knowing they would stand out in a crowd with those coats. The girls felt big, but never better than anyone else. They felt blessed, but always remained humble.

Nicole recalls her mom Florence and Diana's relationship as sisters that drifted apart. The business side of their relationship was what confused them, but the love never changed between either of them. They were like sisters and loved each other with well wishes, but didn't feel a sense of responsibility for the other's affairs as they grew into young women. You were on your own, was the feeling Nicole witnessed from her mom. Florence knew she had to do something, or nothing would happen. She would take time away from everyone at times. Nothing personal. It's just the way she dealt with her periodic obstacles.

When Florence died, Diana Ross asked their grandmother Lurlee if she could have them and raise them. She would take all three with no problem. Their grandmother rejected the offer, because she couldn't let go of her daughter's children, which Diana understood.

Nicole was happy to stay with her dad, grandma, and aunts. She knew her Auntie Boss would see about them. As an adult looking back on everything, Nicole thinks her life would've gone much differently in a more productive and self-fulfilling way had she been left town with her Auntie Boss. She believes she would've gotten therapy and counseling regularly or as needed, which was more than necessary. She would have escaped the molestation and torment from her reckless violating babysitters as well as the rape. Nicole just didn't know any better. The early incidents in her life traumatized her, and began to mold her into who and what she is today. She absolutely loves the person she is, and wouldn't change a thing. She just wants to heal properly and finally. She sends a special thank you to her Auntie Boss for everything. She appreciates the things she did, how she thought about them, and always showed love and concern. It was always felt throughout the Ballard family never to be mistaken. They knew her love to be genuine towards Florence and her children most of all.

CHAPTER CINCO

NICOLE'S MENTIONS

Charles in Charge

In 2001, Nicole met her baby love, Charles. They met on the afternoon of November 12th at a Kmart in Detroit, Michigan. Nicole and her family were just returning home from the award ceremony in New York. A very irritated and frustrated Nicole stepped out of the limo to enter the store for some odd items when she saw Charles.

Mr. Fine had nothing on Mr. Charles. Nicole thought Charles was an attorney by the way he was dressed, but Charles was coming from a funeral. Charles saw Michelle first. He thought she was beautiful. He said a few words to her, but quickly found out that he wasn't financially equipped for Michelle. She told Charles that he should maybe approach her twin sister Nicole, who was not as forward and direct as her. Out steps Nicole, like clockwork. Charles thought to himself, "Wow! Two beautiful ladies."

Both of the twins were beautiful to Charles in their own unique way. Nicole was immediately attracted to Charles. Michelle did not have to say a word, because Nicole claimed him that day and has held on to him ever since. Charles fell in love with Nicole's heart. Charles has never met a woman more selfless than Nicole. He says, "Nicole's heart is huge, and she has consistently cared for others before herself." Charles felt it was no way he could let go of a woman of her kind. Nicole's love and care have kept them afloat for all these years. Charles has been a rock for Nicole and her family. He has shown up for her in many ways for which she will forever be grateful. They have their moments of disagreements, but nothing has been enough to break them.

Faith Evans

By the end of 2010, Nicole was feeling the loss of her loved ones. It was beginning to feel hopeless for many things that stayed on Nicole's mind. Nicole had no aim or idea where to start to heal what she was feeling and dealing with. Sometimes it's unexplainable. She needed something to happen, and fast.

Nicole and her sisters had been approached by different reporters, journalists, and producers from near and far to discuss book and film ideas covering the life of their mom, Florence Ballard, many times. It seemed like the attention was growing more each year. They complied with a few, and were pleased to do so. They were nearly welcoming anything that would help to keep their mother's memory alive. This desperation, coupled with not recognizing fraudulent intent in that industry, caused them to accept an offer without any real understanding. They were none the wiser. A producer approached Nicole and her sisters with an opportunity for them to shine a light on their mother by producing a film telling the story of Florence's life.

This film was based on a book written by someone Nicole disapproves of. This book was the producer's only source of material, which has flaws throughout. Nicole is not interested in giving life to the author by naming him here, because she's personally not a fan of his, as he probably feels the same about her. He has a cordial relationship with her sister Michelle, and that's as far as that goes.

Nicole agreed to this project because it felt like action was finally being taken, even though she wasn't totally approving of the material used.

Nicole and her sisters allowed the producer in charge to take total control with this project. They did well with casting an impressive group of main actors, actors who knew the business a bit more than the hired amateur producers with the idea. The cast did add a production team of their own to try to fill out the holes to collaborate comfortably on a productive honorary project for the family. It did not work out that way. The cast did some digging of their own to confirm and clarify the business end of this project. There were rising rumors and discrepancies that warranted confrontations.

In 2011, Nicci Gilbert, who is one-third of the nationally known 1990's R&B group Brownstone, as well as a successful stage play actor and producer, was cast in this film. After much careful thinking, Gilbert went public, taking to social media sites to announce that Faith Evans, Martha Coolidge (producer), Billie Woodruff (producer), and herself had walked away from this film on their own and that none of them were fired. Gilbert went on to say that Florence 'Blondie' Ballard film was a mess, conducted by ignorant fraudulent producers. Gilbert also showed respect to Florence Ballard's legacy and family throughout that time of disappointment.

Later, it was stated that Jurnee Smollett, the beautifully talented actor from films like *The Great Debaters* and *Eve's Bayou*, would play Florence, replacing Faith Evans. Kandi Burruss, the multi-talented R&B artist from the nationally known girls singing group, Xscape and reality star on The Real Housewives of Atlanta, was prepared to take on the role of Florence Ballard's older sister, Maxine. Nicole never had contact with Smollett or Burruss, and was unsure if it important was real. Nicole and her family began to question the producer's integrity. They experienced some personal incidents with the project management team that gave them pause.

Faith Evans remained silent behind all that went on, and was very saddened by the confusion. She wanted to do it so bad for

Florence and her daughters. Evans never wanted to pull out and would not have had the direction and production been proper. Evans later spoke briefly and vaguely about her not continuing with the Florence Ballard project under the production company's handling. That is when Nicole knew it was a wrap for the film project. It was rather disappointing, because the fraudulent producers actually stayed at the daughter's home and deceived them. Evans made trips to Detroit and spent time with Florence's daughters, even visited their mother Florence's gravesite together with Nicole, Michelle and Lisa.

Faith Evans tried to do what she could to assist in making this film happen. Her heart was pure, and she did not want the project to end. Nicole understood the dynamics of the productions' fraudulent intentions after they were exposed. It was a big disappointment to Nicole, but she was grateful for all of their genuine efforts. Nicole and her sisters built a warm bond with Faith Evans, and are thankful for all of her determination and attempts to bring light to their lives. They know she meant well. The whole experience put a bad taste in Nicole and her family's mouths. Once that project folded, their guards went up, causing them to decline all offers since then.

Flavor Flav

Flavor Flav is someone Nicole cares about deeply, and wants to mention. He has always been a gentleman and respectful to her and her family. She has nothing but love for Flav. She doesn't remember the precise moment she and Flav met, but she's certain that they met at one of the events Motown invited them to. She also remembers meeting Biz Markie and The Fat Boys while hanging backstage with Flav and the other performers before they all went to the Elias Big Boy restaurant downtown on Jefferson Avenue, which is across from Detroit's most famous state park, Belle Isle. Fans were all over them, getting autographs and pictures. The celebs were friendly with the fans and gave off good energy. Nicole's sisters and cousin were working the room as if they were the stars.

Sometime in early 2013, Flav visited Sterling Heights, Michigan, on business related to his once owned chicken shack named "Flavor Flav's Chicken and Ribs." Flav contacted Nicole to invite them to his popular new chicken and ribs restaurant, and to see one another while he was in town. Nicole and her love, Charles, went to visit with Flav. "Flo in the house," sung Flav coming from the back, in the kitchen. This is how Flav greets Nicole always. He calls her "Flo" in reference to the nickname for her mom Florence (Ballard) Chapman. It is Flav's way of honoring Florence and keeping her spirit alive. They visited and talked for a few minutes, before Flav informed his employees to give them whatever they order on the house. A big heart is what Flav possesses, and shows whenever they meet or speak. Thank you, Flavor Flav, for showing love and respect always, from Nicole.

Raymond Gibson

Rest in peace to Florence's cousin, Raymond Gibson, who passed away on March 25, 2018. He was a California resident for many years, after leaving Detroit. He did not visit Detroit much over the past several years after Florence passed, but he always remained in touch with the family, especially Florence's children. Raymond and Florence were first cousins and very close. They spent a lot of time together before, during, and after her success. He was one of the truest people around her. He did not sugar coat things that needed to be said, or just go with the flow. Raymond was always honest with his cousin Florence, and they shared a mutual respect for one another at all times. Raymond was a songwriter, and wrote songs for a few different gospel artists and R&B groups back in the 1960s or so.

Raymond was finishing a book on Florence before his passing. He called to notify Nicole and her sisters of his completion of the book and his plan to release it just weeks before he died. He planned to reach out to the girls again once things were ready. Instead, they received a call stating that God was ready for Raymond and called him home. "Cousin Raymond is no longer with us," was what they were informed.

Jennifer Hudson

Nicole thanks you for acknowledging her mother Florence Ballard while accepting your Golden Globe Award for your awesome portrayal of Effie White in the movie, Dream Girls.

Berry Gordy, Jr.

Nicole understands why so many people have such harsh feelings toward Berry Gordy when it concerns Florence's singing career. The media plays a huge part in sensationalizing its audience. There were disagreements and unfavorable moments between Florence and Gordy in their past, but Nicole did not experience that behavior or treatment from Gordy. Nicole never witnessed anything other than the love between her mother and her Poppa Gordy.

Motown has always taken care of Florence Ballard's daughters. There were times when things got crossed, but they were eventually straightened out. Yes, the girls receive royalty payments. Nicole and her sisters are always personally invited to every event given by Motown, no matter where it's held. The girls are sent travel arrangements when the event is held out of town, and are escorted and catered to. Nicole has lots of love for her 'Poppa Gordy' for always treating them with privilege from childhood, after their mother died, to adulthood, and never forgetting about them.

Thank you, Motown!!!

THE END

FLORENCE

Florence Glenda Ballard Chapman's Timeline

From June 30, 1943 to February 22, 1976 lived a beautiful, boisterous young lady named Florence Glenda Ballard. Before reaching adulthood, Florence began a stardom trail that reached record-breaking heights as a singing trio known worldwide as "The Supremes." The fame, family, and love took this unforgettable talent on a turbulent ride throughout her lifetime.

Background

Florence Ballard's mother, Lurlee Wilson (January 5, 1910 - October 8, 1982), grew up in Rosetta, Mississippi, an unincorporated community. Florence Ballard's father, Jesse Ballard, was born Jesse Lambert in Bessemer, Alabama, in approximately 1910. Very little information on Jesse Ballard has been documented for our findings. Wikipedia explains that Jesse Lambert was a young boy when his grandmother was shot and killed. It's been said that the Lamberts were neighbors of the Ballard family, who adopted Jesse and gave him their last name. Jesse left Bessemer, Alabama, at the age of 13. Sometime after leaving home, Jesse made his way to Rosetta, Mississippi, where he met a stunning 14-year-old young lady named Lurlee Wilson.

The two became an inseparable pair and kindled a young teenage love affair before getting married. Jesse and Lurlee grew tired of the southern blues and decided to move up north for secure jobs and better opportunities.

In 1929, Detroit, Michigan, became their new and final home. Jesse found work at General Motors, while Lurlee cleaned houses for pay. Within three years, Jesse and Lurlee started their family, welcoming a healthy baby boy. Life for the Ballard family had gotten busier for them when two more children were born by 1935, making three children within five years. The family was rapidly expanding, until Jesse and Lurlee were parents to 13 children, as listed: Jesse Jr., Gilbert, Geraldine, Barbara, Jean, Calvin, Cornell, Roy, Pat, Billy, Maxine, Florence, and Linda.

Having children at this rate gave a constant need for expansion, causing the Ballard family to move many times. Jesse made his final move in 1958 when the Ballard family moved into the Brewster Douglas Housing Projects, located at 3526 Saint Antoine Avenue, Detroit, Michigan 48201. Jesse Ballard Sr. was diagnosed with cancer before he moved his family to the projects. He tried to fight the disease as best he could, but it progressed quickly. Sadly, Jesse Ballard died in 1959, just one year after getting his family settled into a new area. Some of what Florence's father taught her remained in her mind and spirit, especially the music lessons and tips.

THE IMPOSSIBLE DREAM

1959

- Florence Ballard, also known as Flo or Blondie, was addressed by her nicknames mostly.
- Florence's singing voice caught the attention of her older sister Maxine's boyfriend, Milton Jenkins. Milton Jenkins was managing talent without paperwork. Milton worked with The Primes, who later moved on to sign with Motown and were renamed The Temptations. While Milton worked with the Primes, he was somewhat interested in finding a female version of the Primes and wanted to name them the Primettes. Florence helped Milton build this group, not knowing that he was preparing the young ladies for a much bigger platform. The Primettes consisted of four young black ladies: Florence Ballard, Mary Wilson, Diana Ross, and Betty McGlown.

1960

- Florence was raped, silenced, and withdrawn for a few months before getting enough strength to get back to living life, but she was never the same afterward.
- The Primettes did all that they could to get Berry Gordy Jr. to sign them to Motown. Filling in for background vocals on recorded tracks was one way The Primettes got inside

the Motown studios, and one step closer to winning over Mr. Gordy.

1961

- Gordy signed the Primettes (Florence, Mary, Diana, and Betty) to Motown. The Primettes became The Supremes after a quick name change.
- Florence dropped out of high school to live out her dream to become a full-time professional singer.

1962

- After eight released singles, the "No-Hit Supremes" was saved by the track titled, "Buttered Popcorn," led by Florence Ballard. This was a local hit that expanded all over the regional Midwest area, but it still was no mainstream hit.

1963

- Martin Luther King Jr. led the largest march in history, *The Great March to Freedom*, on June 23, 1963, in Detroit during the Civil Rights campaign. Florence took great pride in this movement.

1964

Supremes #1 Hits:

- "Where Did Our Love Go?"
- "Come See About Me"
- "Baby Love"

1965

Supremes #1 Hits:

- "Stop in the Name of Love"
- "Back in My Arms Again"
- "I Hear A Symphony"
- Florence purchased her home at 3767 Buena Vista Street in Detroit, Michigan.

1966

Supremes #1 Hits:

- "You Can't Hurry Love"
- "You Keep Me Hangin' On"

1967

- Florence's supreme exit from Motown.
- Cindy Birdsong replaced Florence.

1968

- February 22, 1968, Florence Ballard negotiated a severance settlement with Motown. In March of 1968, Florence arrived to pick up her settlement check. She was informed not to use the Supremes as a reference to compliment her solo career. She later found that demand to be just a threat with no legal merit.
- After a few years of heavy dating, Florence Glenda Ballard married Thomas Chapman in Honolulu on February 29,1968.
- In March, Florence signed with ABC Records.

- ABC released two unsuccessful singles before ultimately deciding to shelve Florence's album rather quickly.
- Florence was concerned about her once label mate, Tammie Terrell, who was suffering from brain tumors, extending over seven brain surgeries.
- Florence continued to perform as a solo artist, opening for Bill Cosby in September at the Chicago's Auditorium Theater.
- Florence and Thomas Chapman became parents to fraternal twins daughters, Nicole and Michelle, on October 13, 1968.
- By the end of 1968, Motown's settlement money was depleted due to Tommy Chapman's financial decisions and Florence's overall mismanagement. It is believed that Tommy's managerial efforts were most sincere, as he would have benefited greatly as well. He was inexperienced, but proceeded to manage without adequate knowledge anyways.

1969

- In January, Florence Chapman performed at one of elected President Nixon's Inaugural balls.

1970

- Florence Chapman was dropped from ABC. The record label was not experienced in marketing Florence's sound. It is assumed that the arrangement made for Florence to never use The Supremes name as a marketing tool for her solo career did more harm than most thought or imagined it would have.

1971

- Florence attempted to recover royalties from Motown that she felt were due to her. To no avail, as her court case was dismissed.
- Florence and Thomas Chapman became parents to a third daughter, baby Lisa.

1972

- Florence filed for divorce, but they later reconciled.
- Motown moved to Los Angeles, California.
- Diana got the leading role in "Lady Sings the Blues."
- Diana left Detroit and the Supremes for good.
- Diana officially went solo.

1973

- Florence lost her brother Jesse Jr. and her brother-in-law, Milton Jenkins, preceding her death.

1974

- Florence stepped back into the spotlight, with the aid and influence of her once Supremes group member, Mary Wilson.
- Florence broke her leg.
- Florence lost her home at 3767 Buena Vista Street in Detroit, Michigan, and her car was also repossessed.

1975

- Florence checked in to Henry Ford Hospital Rehabilitation for alcohol addiction and depression.
- Florence interviewed on The Dave Diles Show.

- Florence Chapman posed for the cover of *Black Stars Magazine*.
- Florence sued her attorney for the misuse of funds under the Talent Management Incorporation, led by Leonard Baun. He was Florence's attorney that helped her fight and win the settlement from Motown. Florence hired Mr. Baun to manage her solo career on the rise with his management company. Leonard Baun was fired for the suspicion of misuse of funds. Baun had other multiple embezzlement charges against him at the time when Florence fired him. He stole the settlement money from Florence. Leonard A. Baun's law license was suspended for two years before the State Bar Grievance Board disbarred him after finding that he used $147,019.14 of Florence's settlement funds for his personal use. Leonard Baun and his sureties repaid every cent to Florence.
- Florence bought another home at 17071 Shaftsbury Street in Detroit, Michigan.

1976

- February 22, 1976, Florence Chapman dies.

ACKNOWLEDGMENTS

I am grateful for my existence giving me the opportunity to be great while doing great things. I'm grateful for my parents (Gregory L. Williamson Sr. & Dorothy Williamson/Pinkston) making me and raising me while exampling greatness. The impact you two made on my life is as real as my inherited traits for you. At your proudest moment of me, know that I am always reaching for more, just like you.

I am grateful for my stepmom Janice Williamson for being nothing less than loving and supportive of all I do. I love you to life. My husband William Smith, I appreciate you for tolerating and respecting the time it took to complete something so satisfying to my soul, and that means more to me than I could ever explain. I am blessed to have your undying love, as you have mine. My brothers Melvin Pinkston and Marvin Adams, for being the examples of intelligence and creativity exuding with extraordinary talents.

My sons Gregory Williamson II, Malik, Tahj, and Justice Smith. You keep me on my toes. I promise to keep the bar high and show you that you can do it. I promise to continue being an example of success with everything I do. Thank you for your support and understanding when my attention was shared; your hearts were never spared. It makes me feel invincible. Lenoris Allen, my cousin, my sister, my best friend. Thank you for always having my back, even when we disagree. We are so opposite, but the same. It's weird, but natural. I love how we stay in the same fields. Us reaching our ultimate goals together will happen inevitably. Vanessa (Brown) Bonds, there is nothing I can't count on you for. Your love and support are always the same. You mean the world to me, as you already know. Connie Shanai Brown, I love and miss you so much. I did it!!! I know you are proud of me, and we will continue to share my journey spiritually. Deantu Brown, Kendriek, Tony, Alonzo, Anthony, Tonya, Andrea, Kassandra, Amanda, Aundre, Tyrone, Deshawn, Darren, Christine (Too Too) Cherisse (Wee Wee), Aunt Patty, Lula (Lay Lay), Big Ty... Tawayne, Al (50) and my entire Brown family in Pontiac, I love y'all so much for showing up and showing out for me always. One call is all it takes for my family to load up and pack a venue. Major supporters with all that I do. You all make me look big. I love you to the moon and back times infinity for that. Anquinette Rollins, I appreciate you so much. You have always been a supportive factor, whether you are present or not. I can't thank you enough for that. Grandma Celeste Williamson, I know you're with me always, Ma Elizabeth Smith and Mary Gaines, thank you for genuine love. I love you always. Aunt Jackie, thank you for a wonderful relationship, listening to all of my ups and downs along my journey to success. Thank you for loving and supporting me. You are my heart.

Ewanda Wyndella, my big sis who taught me and paved the way. Thank you. I love you to life. Rita Adams, you the bomb sis! You got me even when it's a challenge. A special thank you to Camesha Coneal and Daniel (Jack) Williamson, for jumping in and helping me write the screenplay for the film, *In the Name of Love*, #writersforflo. I have not forgotten about you. Your work is not in vain. Uncle Jack, you are the coolest, most loving and supportive, and no one compares. Aunt Dedtch, I appreciate you having my back, and loving me unconditionally. Thank you and Uncle Bill for diving right in when I needed you, no questions asked.

Janet, Natalie, and Novella, thanks for the love and support. My bestie Shawndell, since age four, until infinity and beyond. Sonya Ross, since age five or six, no matter what, we support. Jay Lamont, thank you for thinking of me for the *In the Name of Love* film project for Florence Ballard Chapman that we started and completed the

ACKNOWLEDGMENTS

script for. Thank you for setting the tone with Nicole and De'Juan. They believed you and accepted me. I appreciate that.

De'Juan, thank you for all the trust, loyalty, respect, and honor that you dedicated to me. Thank you for believing in me totally. You make me feel big, nephew. I will not disappoint. The love you show for your grandmother keeps her smiling down on you, I'm sure. To keep someone's name alive with all you do is the most honorable token you can give her. I feel like I'm a part of your mission. I'm honored. Michelle Chapman, I have nothing but respect for you. Your honesty is appreciated. You don't sugar coat anything. That's a trait I appreciate. I want you to know that the talk we had, I heard you, I understood you, and I respected your position. I decided to say less and do more. To present a finished product, uplifting your mother's name was my goal. Nicole Chapman, I have been blessed with a sister and friend. I treasure our journey and cherish our bond. I love you sis! Nicholas Lamont Stiles and Jim Saphin, thank you for offering your time in assisting me. I totally appreciate you. Braden Hunter and Kim Clarke, I added you to the credits because I learned a little more from reading your articles and connected some pieces to the puzzle that I was missing.

The Fans

Florence (Ballard) Chapman still has a large fan base in the United States and the United Kingdom. It's moving to read the comments fans leave on blog sites, expressing their love for her. Some share memories as they reminisce on moments in their lives that connected them to Florence's music. Her life and career were cut short, but her fans live on and help keep her name alive. This means the world to Nicole. Thank you.

- Blog site: www.Soulful Detroit.com
- Blog Title: Florence Ballard's Daughter's
- Florence_ballard_fanpage/Instagram
- Florenceglendaballard/Instagram
- Florence Ballard Bio Pic/Facebook
- Florence Ballard Forever Faithful/Facebook
- Florence Ballard Times/Facebook
- Florence Ballard Archives/Facebook
- Florence Ballard/Facebook
- The Supremes Fan page/Facebook
- The Supremes Fan Page/Instagram

ACKNOWLEDGMENTS

Nicholas Lamont Stiles

A dedicated, consistent fan of The Supremes with a special love for Florence (Ballard) Chapman. Nicholas runs The Supremes Fan Page on Facebook and Instagram, keeping Florence's memory alive. Mr. Stiles posts will keep you informed and updated on The Supremes' legacy. Nicholas met Nicole and her sisters at the R&B Hall of Fame White Party on June 22, 2019, in Detroit,

Michigan. Nicholas also met other Supreme group members that night. Nicholas remembers Nicole being the nicest person ever, and she told him she loves him for loving her mother. He was touched and ended that night with the most grateful and emotional ride home. He will never forget them or that night.

Jim Saphin

Jim Saphin is one of Florence Ballard Chapman's most loyal fans from the The United Kingdom. He became the President and secretary of the first fan club for The Supremes in Great Britain from 1966 until 1970. Jim met Florence once in 1965 during the Motown Revue Tour. Jim remembers Florence being very gracious to him, and kindly signed an autograph for him. Unfortunately, in the 1960s, cameras were not as accessible as today, leaving Jim this wonderful memory captured internally. Jim has memories with The Supremes as a whole with pictures and stories about his time following their career on his websit. Jim was labeled "Motown Jim" during his four years of following The Supremes. Jim is also a singer. His sound is smooth, comforting, and jazzy, in my opinion. You can find his music on his website @jimsaphin.com

REFERENCES

- "To Be Loved: The Music the Magic the Memories of Motown" by Berry Gordy Jr. December 1, 1995
- "Backstage at the Graystone" by Kim Clarke, 2017
- How the Cruel & Unforgiving Streets of Detroit Swallowed Up Reggie Harding by Branden Hunter, 2017
- Dave Diles Show Interview with Florence Ballard, 1975
- Pan-African News Wire (PANW), Abayomi Azikiwe December 30, 2006.

CREDITS

- Cover Photo: Uno 220
- Cover Design: Kom Poo Pie Publishing, LLC.
- Interior Design: Kom Poo Pie Publishing, LLC.
- Printing: Kom Poo Pie Publishing, LLC.
- Photo Images: Dedtra J. Bell, Kali Williamson, William Bell Jr., Jet Magazine, The Detroit Free Press, Soul Newsletter, Nicole Chapman, Nychole Smith
- Book Design: Uno 220, Kom Poo Pie Publishing, LLC., Fame Up Entertainment
- Editor: Tina Luckett, Script Writt, Kom Poo Pie Publishing LLC.
- Proofread: Polgarus Studio, Tina Luckett, Script Writt, #Nycholekwroteit
- Publishing: Kom Poo Pie Publishing LLC.
- Article: The Detroit Free Press, 1976 (Introduction)
- Article: Jet Magazine, 1975, 1976 (Introduction)
- Article: Soul Newsletter, 1967, 1976 (Introduction)
- Interview inserts: Dave Diles, Ebony

ABOUT THE AUTHOR

Who is Uno 220?

Shawniqua Nychole Williamson - Smith, aka Uno 220, is a female rap artist. Uno 220 (second to none) released her first single titled, "Sippin'" in 2013, featuring Ro Spit. Uno 220 has performed different music showcases on locally, but her greatest and most honorable performances were with the Jackson family. In 2013, Uno 220 met Michael Jackson's first cousin, Keith Jackson. Uno 220 was invited to a celebration that the family was soon having in honor of the then late Michael Jackson, remembering him on the date he died, June 25th. Uno 220 met Michael's father's side of his family and performed for them and close friends at the celebration. Keith Jackson also performed with his band, "The Triple Dose Band."

Uno 220 also performed at Michael Jackson's birthday celebration outside 2300 Jackson Street in Gary, Indiana. Mrs. Katherine Jackson celebrated her son's birthday, August 29th, there every year for almost a decade consecutively. Uno 220 extends a huge thank you to Keith, Mrs. Katherine Jackson and Sandy Christmas of ABC Television Network for adding her involvement last minute.

Uno 220 networked her way into video and movie production. She co-produced videos under the training of Producer Sareta Cheathem for Detroit's own superstars, K'Jon, Dwele, and Seven the General, with collaborations from Trina, the baddest b!tch, and Phife from "A Tribe Called Quest," all directed by Darren Brown of DM Films. In 2012, Uno 220 worked with Sareta and Darren on *Winnerz* the movie, starring Glenn Plummer and Christian Keyes shot in Cleveland, Ohio. Uno 220 was a part of the production team, learning more about scriptwriting and how to transfer a written story to a screen of any type. The on-set experience was indescribably gratifying, which lead Uno 220 to becoming a free-lance producer, writing skits, standup comedy, and screenplays for future projects. Uno 220 is a senior writer for the online magazine, Fame Up Magazine on Facebook, under the signature, #Nycholekwroteit. Most of her work on Fame Up Magazine has been Black History motivated. Writing is a creative lane for Uno 220, where she tackles different styles, enjoying them all, especially embracing biography. It's another form of therapy appearing to supply certain healing that comes with the completion of a book in this genre for herself and others. Uno 220 welcomes the exceptional growth with every accomplishment. She expresses her growth through more in-depth understanding, compassion, and wisdom.

FLORENCE BALLARD CHAPMAN SPEAKS

Florence discussed how she felt about getting back into the music business at ABC Records in 1969 in an interview with Ebony.

"I didn't ever intend to get back into show business. I thought I'd make a few investments and just sort of stay home and take care of Tommy and the kids. But you know my fans get my telephone number somehow and they call me up and ask what I'm doing and why I don't sing again. So I decided to give it a try. If things don't work out I can always come back here and enjoy my house [...] I'm sort of like a—well, like Richard Nixon you might say. Remember how everybody thought he was all washed up? They thought he was out of it—through. But Nixon didn't think it; he believed in Richard Nixon. Now look where he is today. Same thing with me: I believe in Florence Ballard. I believe I can make it. Just because I'm not with The Supremes doesn't mean that I have to sit here in Detroit and dry up. I could have half a dozen flops and I'd still believe in me. I wonder if people know how many flops The Supremes had before we made it big?"

"It felt great to be recording again [...] it felt really great, I liked it a lot" and said ABC had hired

> "these three girls to do background: they were really good too, very good. And the music, they had gotten a band, session men, musicians who play for records [...] I liked the tunes, sure did, and my voice hadn't declined. The records sound great to me, and to a lot of people."

Florence's interview with Dave Dile in 1975.

This snippet covers Florence speaking on how it felt for her to look at old pictures of her with Dianna Ross and Mary Wilson and how listening to "Put on a Happy Face,' recorded while she was a Supreme affected her in that moment as well as in her life.

> "Ummm, well Looking at the pictures umm looking at it really bout seconds, but uhh for me Mary and Diane.... uhh that's why I feel lost listening to the record cause it took a long time to want to listen to them again. I was in such a... uhh mind uhh just mentally uhh well I had mental anguish and uhh a whole bunch of other mental problems. Um... It was bitterness, and ummm just hearing the record, I guess inside I wanted to still be there and I couldn't and it seemed to just... in other words tear me up inside."

HAPPY HEAVENLY 77TH BIRTHDAY

FLORENCE GLENDA BALLARD CHAPMAN

JUNE 30, 2020

On this day, Nicole Chapman and her family began their celebration for her mother's 77th year at the Detroit Memorial Cemetery, located in Warren, Michigan. They visited with Florence and her mother, Lurlee Ballard, who rests right next to one another. The family shared memories of their own, bringing about laughter as well as sadness. The weather peaked at 84 degrees with the humidity, making it feel like 90 plus degrees. Due to the Coronavirus (Covid-19), masks were worn, and some "social distancing" was maintained amongst them all on that beautiful sunny day as they embraced the moment.

Pepper (the pup) engaged with Florence and her mother, Lurlee's gravesite, as if she was a return visitor and knew whom she was visiting. Pepper seemed excited to visit Florence's gravesite by way of her odd behavior rolling around and sliding through the grass the way she did. Her movements were hilariously entertaining, while mysteriously accurate when giving direct attention to the two gravesites. Pepper is the exact breed of dog that Florence Ballard Chapman had when Nicole was a child. Nicole remembers her mother's dog, "Sugar Pie" to look exactly like her dog, "Pepper." Sugar Pie died of old age before Florence died. Pepper was randomly given to Nicole out of the blue one day. It was strange yet welcoming when she received Pepper.

At Florence Chapman's gravesite, together for the first time, Nicole and I asked for Florence's guidance and blessing as they embark on this book project and others to follow. After forty-four challenging years of Nicole missing her mother, the pain never got easier for her and her family. Florence Glenda Ballard was born in 1943 and would have celebrated 33 years of life on Earth and more, had not the tragic, unfortunate moment of Florence's expiration took place on February 22, 1976. Florence is deeply missed by her loved ones and cherished with memories. Florence lives within her family.

Pepper the pup

Nicole Chapman, her nephew Darryl Chapman
& her daughter Florence Chapman

Nicole & Charles Arnett

Nicole & Nychole (Uno 220)

Mary Wilson is asking EVERYONE to write in to the USPS STAMP COMMITTEE and ask them to pass the official FLORENCE BALLARD stamp!

Send your letters to :
Stamp Development
Citizens' Stamp Advisory Committee
475 L'Enfant Plaza SW, Room 3300
Washington, DC 20260-3501